Y0-CDH-812

Martha Graham

Martha Graham

by
Kathilyn Solomon Probosz

A People in Focus Book

DILLON PRESS
Parsippany, New Jersey

Photo Credits

Front Cover: © Barbara Morgan/Morgan Press.

Back Cover: Angus McBean Photograph/Harvard Theatre Collection.

Courtesy of The Estate of Martha Graham: 16, 79, 86. Sara Krulwich/NYT Pictures: 171. Martha Graham Dance Company: 6, 55, 105. © Barbara Morgan/ Morgan Press: 68, 77, 95. New York Public Library: 48, 167, 33 (photo by Harsook), 59 and 66 (photos by Soichi Sunami). Martha Swope © Time Inc.: 117. ©1994 Martha Swope: 127, 141. © 1989 Martha Swope: 153. Jim Wilson/ New York Times Pictures: 163.

Library of Congress Cataloging-in-Publication Data
Probosz, Kathilyn Solomon.
   Martha Graham / by Kathilyn Solomon Probosz.—1st ed.
     p. cm.—(People in focus)
   Includes bibliographical references and index.
   ISBN 0-87518-568-1   ISBN 0-382-24961-5 pbk
   1. Graham, Martha. 2. Dancers—United States—Biography. 3.
Choreographer—United States—Biography. 4. Modern dance. I. Title. II.
Series: People in focus book.
GV1785.G7P76 1994
792.8'028'092–dc20   94-8992
[B]

Summary: A biography of Martha Graham, one of the most influential and successful artists in the world of modern dance.

Published by Dillon Press, an imprint of Silver Burdett Press.
A Simon & Schuster Company
299 Jefferson Road, Parsippany NJ 07054

First Edition

Printed in Mexico

10 9 8 7 6 5 4 3 2 1

/Contents

Chapter / One

Destined to Dance

"There is only one of you in the world, just one, and if that is not fulfilled, then something has been lost."[1]

When Martha Graham said those words, she spoke from her own experience. She started studying dance later in life than did most professionals. People had told her that she did not have a dancer's body or look. Yet she believed that if she didn't express her unique self through dancing, something would be lost.

And against the odds, Martha did become a dancer—not just any dancer but the star of a famous company. Then, at the peak of her popularity, she gave up fame and fortune to create her own dances and start her own company. No one thought she would succeed. She had no money. In the beginning, she had very little support from the dance world and she enraged the critics. Through it all, Martha kept working, and bit by bit, people began to recognize her for the genius she was.

Martha Graham pioneered a new art called modern dance. She established a system of movement that was named after her and is used to this day. Her work revolutionized the way people look at dance. In her own time, Martha became a legend and was heralded as one of the finest modern artists of the twentieth century. It happened only because she didn't merely intend to fulfill her dreams; she made them happen. This is her story.

❖ ❖ ❖

At the time Martha was born, on May 11, 1894, there was no such thing as modern dance. But on that special day, Dr. George Graham may have danced around the bed of his wife, Jenny, as he rejoiced at the birth of their first child.

Even as a toddler, Martha loved music. It was music that led her to give her first performance. She was only about two years old, and her middle sister, Mary, had just been born. The family wasn't at a theater but at church when Martha heard a song she loved. She began wriggling to the music in her mother's lap. Her mother tried to quiet her, but Martha kept squirming so much that her mother finally set her down. Instantly, Martha headed for the aisle and began dancing down it in her white dress. The church congregation watched in shock, not because she showed a remarkable talent but because no one had ever done such a thing in church before. To Martha, that didn't matter. She had to dance—so she would dance!

Around this time, her mother realized that in Martha's case, appearances were very deceiving. No matter how many times Mrs. Graham dressed her little girl in white gloves and delicate white dresses, they simply could not conceal the wildness lurking within Martha. And white dresses were not practical in Martha's hometown of Allegheny (now part of Pittsburgh), Pennsylvania, anyway. The area's main industry was mining coal, and as the coal was removed, it coated the city in thick black ash. At that time, coal was used to heat houses and power trains and factories across the United States. To protect themselves from breathing the unhealthy black soot, the Graham girls wore veils over their heads.

"I remember walking on Main Street as a

young girl, a veil covering my eyes, my nose, and my mouth,"[2] wrote Martha in her autobiography *Blood Memory*. She liked wearing the veil because she said its thin gauzy fabric transformed the world into a land of mystery.

The Grahams, direct descendants of Miles Standish, who had helped establish the first American colony at Plymouth, were well-respected in their town. Martha's father, Dr. George Greenfield Graham, treated people who were suffering from mental illness. His office was on the ground floor of the family's two-story house. "It [the office] felt different from any room I had ever been in,"[3] wrote Martha. With its walls lined with books; its microscope and other equipment for scientific study; medical paraphernalia; and the strangers visiting each day, it was a place of discovery for a young girl. Encouraged by Martha's curiosity, Dr. Graham took the time to explain his work to her.

Dr. Graham's first step toward healing people was to pay close attention to the movement of their bodies. He explained that the body's movement not only revealed what a person was feeling but also gave priceless clues as to the cause of the ailment. In a sense, he acted as a detective whose job was to ferret out the illnesses hurting the bodies and minds of his patients. And he had a very keen eye for this kind of work.

Martha, however, apparently thought she was the exception to Dr. Graham's eagle eyes. Once she did something wrong and dared to lie about it. Dr. Graham looked down at her and said sternly, "Martha, you are lying."

Martha was ashamed and confessed on the spot. How did her father catch her, she wanted to know. Dr. Graham explained that he could see her lie in the tenseness of her body and the fact that she was standing far straighter than usual. Her body revealed to him the turmoil she was feeling over not telling the truth. "Movement never lies," he said.

This idea intrigued Martha. She quit lying and began to observe family, friends, and strangers very closely, sometimes a little too closely. Once, when a patient came for dinner, Martha stared at her the whole time. While she probably caused the woman to feel a bit uncomfortable, she observed that the woman was slouching, fidgeting, and rarely looking up from her plate. Most visitors sat straight, smiled, and made eye contact with their hosts. Luckily, Martha's manners were too good to directly ask the woman what was wrong. She waited until the woman left and then questioned her father. He said that the woman was very sick and her body was telling her so, just as Martha had suspected.

Already, Martha had acquired the gift of understanding what people's true intentions and feelings are, including their deepest secrets. Paying attention to the way others moved helped Martha to understand them without their saying a single word. This knowledge helped her later, when she became a dancer and choreographer. She could even tell if a person had what it takes to be a dancer just by having her walk across the studio floor saying, "This is my name."[4] Many called Martha's ability supernatural.

It wasn't magic. It was based on the lesson she learned from her father as a child. How could someone as young as Martha pay such full attention and integrate so much information from others? First, she found people fascinating. Second, Martha's parents demanded that she do everything to the best of her ability, whether it was her schoolwork, her dress for an outing, or her ironing of white handkerchiefs, a task that her grandmother supervised and one that Martha didn't like very much. If she left even the tiniest wrinkle in a handkerchief, her grandmother dropped it back into a bucket of water, and

Martha had to start again. Martha's grandmother helped her develop a penchant for perfection. "You must look for the truth,"[5] Martha's father would say. He encouraged her to think for herself and to get to the bottom of things, not by asking someone for help but by finding out for herself.

That's how Martha developed a large vocabulary. If she came across an unfamiliar word, she looked it up in the dictionary instead of asking her parents to define it. If she heard a new word, she repeated it over and over until she got the pronunciation right, and she never used a word if she wasn't certain of its meaning. The dictionary was one of her two favorite books, the Bible was the other, because its amazing stories sparked her imagination. She also enjoyed looking up large words and breaking them down by syllables. In this way she discovered the meaning of each of the word parts, as well as the origins.

Her play enabled her to understand the very essence of a word's meaning and also made her appear very clever. As a choreographer, she used this process of breaking things down into their basic meanings to help her create her dances. She started with the germ of an idea and worked her way out to create a form for it.

From her father, Martha also learned that

being true to oneself was more important than being popular. For example, one day in church her father disagreed with the minister's lecture. Even though all the other parishioners were listening in silence with complete attention, Dr. Graham stood up, called the minister a liar, and herded his family out of the church. To speak up in this way was very brave, for people were expected to accept what the minister said without question. Dr. Graham, however, knew that to be a healthy individual, he must stand up for his beliefs. This made a strong impression on Martha, who followed in her father's footsteps. All her life she did not hesitate to say what she meant. She was fearless, and though some of her stands did not win her any friends, she didn't let this bother her.

Martha's mother, Jane (called Jenny), supported Dr. Graham wholeheartedly. She was bright and well-read and often discussed his mysterious cases with him. Jenny was his partner in all aspects of his life. This was during a time in which women didn't even have the right to vote. Very few played a role in politics, business, or the arts. Yet because of her parents' example, Martha grew up believing that women could do everything that men could do.

Jenny was very pretty, dressed stylishly, and

wore her hair pulled back and up. When Martha grew up, she adopted that hairstyle for her own. She respected her mother so much that each year on her own birthday, she sent her mother a telegram or note that read, "On this, my birthday, thank you for my life."[6]

Martha's nanny, Elizabeth Prendergast (known as Lizzie), was another important person in Martha's life. Lizzie had joined the Graham household soon after Martha was born. Early one morning, the Irishwoman had come knocking at their door. With a crying Martha in her hands, Jenny answered. Lizzie introduced herself and said that Dr. Graham had saved her life some years before, and she had been unable to pay him. In lieu of payment, she had promised that she would return once Dr. Graham had a wife and child to help care for them. Jenny welcomed the help, and Lizzie remained with the Graham family all of her life.

Lizzie's sweet voice would waken the girls each morning with a song. And she knew all the popular ones. She was a storyteller and loved the theater. Best of all, she loved Martha, Mary, and their youngest sister, Georgia (nicknamed Geordie), who had been born on March 1, 1900.

Just as Martha hung on her handsome father's every word, she savored the stories that Lizzie

Martha Graham, age 9

shared. Thus inspired by Lizzie, she and her sisters used their mother's scarves, veils, fabrics, and costume jewelry and transformed themselves into exotic characters in plays. Martha had no clue that the fun she was having was laying the groundwork for her expert ability to design costumes and to stage dances as an adult. She made props, used a bedsheet as a curtain, and finally, she wrote invitations instructing her family and Lizzie to come to the playroom at a certain hour. When they all arrived, the theater performance began.

Martha created such realistic sets that the playroom could become a kingdom suffering under the curse of a wicked magician; the deep, dark forest from the story of Hansel and Gretel; or a laboratory full of strange inventions. But when Martha turned her dollhouse into Little Red Riding Hood's home, she went too far. She actually lit a fire in the toy fireplace. Lizzie was not invited to this performance but luckily she smelled smoke, came to Martha's room, and put the fire out.

When Martha finally saw her first real theater performance, she was amazed. "Ah, there's a world, there's a world. I am going to find it!" she thought.[7] To Martha, it was a world that had no boundaries, because it was in the imagination. Martha's imagination, power of concentration, overwhelming curiosity, and desire to achieve perfection were traits that served her well all her life.

When Martha was 12 years old, she gained yet another person whom she could invite to her own plays. His name was William, and he was the newest addition to the Graham family. William was baptized in a crystal bowl that had been Martha's grandmother's. Since William was the only boy in the family, Martha and her sisters gave him lots of love and attention. Unfortunately, when he was 18 months old, William died of meningitis.

Curtains in the once-happy Graham household were kept closed. There was no more singing or theater. To help get over their grief, the Grahams decided to move. The spring after William died, they exchanged the black sooty air of western Pennsylvania for the clean, clear air and ocean breezes of Santa Barbara, California, on the coast of the Pacific Ocean. The Grahams thought that starting over in such a different place would help ease their pain over losing William.

For Martha, who was now 14, even the Spanish name *Santa Barbara* sounded exotic. In contrast to Allegheny, Santa Barbara was a growing town full of wide-open spaces, sunlight, and people from all over the world. Fragrant flowers and cactuses grew year-round in the warm climate. The dolphins that lived in the ocean fascinated Martha. She studied the way their arching gray bodies gracefully leaped into the air and then smoothly disappeared back into the ocean. She loved all animals, but these gentle creatures seemed especially magical to her.

Martha blossomed in Santa Barbara. Out of doors, away from the coal dust, she could not help giving herself over to the joy of being free, a trait that continued to alarm her mother. During visits to the Pacific Ocean's cliffs, Martha ran as fast as she could, arms outstretched. If she fell, she'd pick herself up and start running again just as quickly. "The sunlight was so rich, the landscape so clear, I drank in as much of it as my body could encompass,"[8] wrote Martha.

Once, when the family visited the olive groves that Dr. Graham owned with a partner, Mrs. Graham left Martha outside, thinking she was going to be skipping rope. Martha began exploring instead. In particular, one tree with a branch about seven feet off the ground attracted her. Her mother happened to glance outside and spotted Martha. Her daughter was jumping rope all right, high off the ground on the branch of an olive tree—until Mrs. Graham got to her.

Probably to Martha's disappointment, she was for-
bidden to go out unsupervised for a while after the
incident.

Mrs. Graham kept trying to rein her daughter
in, but Martha was not interested in becoming a
proper lady. She said that she behaved exactly as
she wanted to. Her father, in a sense, encouraged
her. He used to say, "If you're going to make a
scandal, Martha, make it a big one!"[9] She would
go on to do so, revolutionizing the world of dance
in the process.

Martha's younger sisters idolized her, and
while she was unquestionably their leader, she felt
very different from them. She didn't say so then,
but in an interview when she was an adult she
recalled how she thought they were so beautiful.
"Then there was little old slit-eyed me. I was not
the pretty one."[10]

From that interview, it was clear that as a
teenager Martha wanted to appear attractive, as
most people do. Her feelings that she wasn't,
however, didn't stop her from being brave, confident, and full of dignity. These qualities were far
more important than physical appearance, for they
made people like and respect Martha. And the
same qualities helped her excel in school, scholas-
tically and athletically. She captained the girls'

basketball team and edited the school magazine, the *Olive and Gold*.

Her curiosity about the world outside the Graham household continued to grow. In Santa Barbara, there were people of Spanish descent, Chinese and Japanese immigrants, and Native Americans. They lived very different lives from Martha and her sisters, and attended different churches. Lizzie once took her to a mass at a Catholic church that was also a mission for Native Americans. After the Catholic service ended, the doors of the church were thrown open. In the bright sunlight of the courtyard outside, Martha could see Native Americans on horses shooting guns into the air. Far from being an attack on the worshippers, the gunshots were the signal that visitors were welcome in the area. Martha stepped into the sandy courtyard and watched as the Native Americans performed their own religious service, a costumed dance of worship.

Native American ceremonial dancing made an impact on Martha that lasted all her life. From it she learned that there were countless ways to express one's spirituality. She would later study the southwestern Native American cultures, drawing inspiration from their dances to create her own. And it wasn't only the ceremonial rituals of the

Native Americans that inspired her. The rituals,
the saints, and the costumes of the clergy in the
Catholic churches she visited with Lizzie also
impressed her. They were much more elaborate
and theatrical than those of Martha's own
Presbyterian church.

It was after a visit to a Catholic mission that
Martha saw a poster on Main Street that caught
her eye. She moved closer. The poster showed a
woman named Ruth St. Denis sitting cross-legged
on a small platform and wearing an exotic
costume. Her arms were cluttered with bracelets
and in her fluffy white hair was a crown of jewels.
Her face radiated a look of total peace. This
woman appeared to be no less dignified, confident,
and respectable than Martha's own mother,
despite her flamboyant costume.

Martha read the ad with increasing interest. It
was for a recital in Los Angeles, about three hours
away from where Martha's family lived. Ruth St.
Denis was a new kind of star on the American
horizon, a dancer. Her dances, which she performed barefoot, imitated those of other cultures.
America at this time was becoming as interested
in the cultures of other nations as Martha was
about almost everything.

People were just beginning to consider dance

as a form of entertainment. The costumes of some of these new dancers revealed more of the body than what was considered appropriate. And usually the music, sets, and costumes were more important than the performance of the dancers, who served almost as ornaments on the stage. Classical ballet had only recently made its arrival in America, and it was becoming popular because of Anna Pavlova, a popular ballerina from Russia.

Martha didn't know anything about dance, but she knew that she had to see Miss St. Denis perform. And when Martha knew what she wanted, nothing could change her mind. She pestered her father so much to take her that he finally agreed. He must have realized how important the concert was to Martha, for he purchased a dress and hat for her to wear to it. On the night of the concert, he pinned a corsage of violets on her dress and the two traveled in an elegant horse-drawn carriage to the theater.

Martha and her father took their seats. The theater lights dimmed, and the auditorium grew silent. Then Ruth St. Denis appeared in a spot-light. Martha watched as Miss Ruth, as she was called, became an Indian priestess charming a snake. During a dance about ancient Egypt, it was as if Martha herself were there.

Martha was transformed by the experience. Her destiny was decided on the spot—she would be a dancer. "I was caught forever,"[11] Martha said later. She wanted to be a part of the dancing world of Miss Ruth and decided she would do anything to become a dancer. At 17, Martha had found the outlet to express her wildness, intelligence, and creativity.

The year was 1911, and dance, like theater, was still not a respectable profession. While most Americans liked to watch theater, they didn't like performers too much. They felt performers, with their wild costumes and their traveling shows, should not be trusted.

Martha thought quite the opposite, but she couldn't meet Miss Ruth just yet. She first had to finish high school. She quit playing basketball, though, because she didn't want to injure her legs. She replaced that activity by joining the school's dramatic and debating clubs. She focused even more diligently on her piano study, too. After she graduated, she chose to study at the closest thing to a dance school that existed at that time—the Cumnock School of Expression, a theatrical college.

In Martha's second year of study, on August 11, 1914, her father died. Martha was heartbroken. Without her father, "everything again seemed as dark as Pittsburgh," Martha wrote.[12] This time, there wasn't enough money for the Grahams to start over. The whole family went through a dark period. Martha made herself continue in college, because she knew her father would have wanted her to.

Two years after her father's death, Martha heard that Miss Ruth and her husband, Ted Shawn, had established a dance school. She quickly made plans to visit the school and finally start learning how to dance. And so it was that five years after she had first seen Miss Ruth perform, an excited Martha Graham crossed through the doors of the Ruth St. Denis School of Dancing and Related Arts to begin to fulfill her dream of becoming a dancer.

Chapter / Two

Dancing Against the Odds

The Ruth St. Denis School of Dancing and the Related Arts, called Denishawn after St. Denis and her husband, Ted Shawn, was located in a large, airy, Spanish-style estate at the very top of a hill. Martha saw that there was room to run, soar, leap, fall, and roll amid the fragrant trees, lush gardens, and lily-filled ponds. And the courses Denishawn offered filled her with even more excitement.

The curriculum included classical ballet; Greek, Spanish, Native American, East Indian, Egyptian, and Japanese dance; decorative use of the body; piano lessons; lighting; makeup; designing and making costumes, jewelry, and props; Red Cross auxiliary; yoga; art and philosophy lectures; and anything remotely related to dance. There was no school like Miss Ruth's anywhere in the world.

Miss Ruth's philosophy was that dance includes all the ways that humans have moved rhythmically to express themselves—in any century, in any country, in any situation. She believed that the body was a temple, that dance was a religious experience, and that the development of the students' minds was as important as that of their bodies.

Miss Ruth and Isadora Duncan, another pioneer in the modern-dance movement, were among the world's first artists who became known as modern dancers. Both became famous during a time when women wore tight corsets under their dresses to make their waists appear as small as possible. Sometimes the corsets were laced so tight that women had trouble breathing normally. In contrast to this physical imprisonment, Miss Ruth's and Isadora's costumes flowed freely and revealed the body's natural lines. The artists' performances demonstrated the body's beauty in dances that were artistically pleasing. The dancers also showed a lot of women who suffered in suffocating corsets that it was possible to dress more naturally and not be shunned because of it.

Martha couldn't wait to meet Miss Ruth. But first she was taken to a small room. It was empty except for a white grand piano. A man smoking a cigar, his eyes half closed, was seated at the piano. Then a woman with fluffy white hair entered, her garments flowing about her.

It was Miss Ruth, the woman Martha had dreamed of meeting for five long years! Miss Ruth sat down, smiled, and said, "Dance for me."[1]

For probably one of the rare times in her life, Martha hesitated. Although inwardly she must have been nervous, she calmly said, "Miss St. Denis, I have never danced before and don't know anything about it."

But Miss Ruth insisted. Martha took a deep breath and then threw herself into her performance. She moved wildly as if her life depended on it. When she finished, she waited eagerly for Miss Ruth to respond. But all Miss Ruth said was, "Thank you." She had decided that Martha was not right for her company.

The man who played the piano, though, had also been watching Martha dance. Though he said nothing, his reaction had been very different from Miss Ruth's. He saw something very special in Martha. She had kept her composure and had been honest. She had thrown herself into the dance and performed with more sincerity and passion than he had ever seen, despite knowing nothing about dance. And she had done it wholeheartedly in front of America's most famous dancer. That took guts.

The piano player was Louis Horst. He later became Martha's composer and a source of invaluable support for her. Miss Ruth didn't ask Louis's opinion, though. But since she saw that Martha wanted so badly to enroll in the school, Miss Ruth told her husband, "You take her in your classes, Teddy dear. I don't know what to do with her."[2]

Miss Ruth and Ted felt that Martha's facial features; hair color, which was brown, not blond; and even her body were not right for the company. Not only that, but at 22, Martha was much older than the other students, who were teenagers. Understandably, she didn't quite fit in with them. She sat apart from the others in class. Many of the young dancers thought she was unfriendly. They were wrong. Martha's behavior was a consequence of her desire not to miss any of the lesson. Her effort showed in the intensity of her dance, which others began to notice and admire.

Martha loved everything about the school. Nothing was off-limits. Her wildness and her desire to experiment and to rebel, which her mother had so rigorously tried to keep under wraps, flourished through dance and the school's freewheeling atmosphere. Soon her body was capable of expressing anything that her teachers demanded. She became aware of the "frenzy which animates the dancer's body frame from within,"[3] as she called it.

Despite Martha's progress, though, she watched helplessly as other students were chosen to join the company instead of her. Still she did not give up—not when she was given the job of teaching children, not when she was given the job of helping take care of Miss Ruth's ailing mother. All this she did and more.

Martha later said she was terrified that Miss Ruth would send her away. Martha so loved dance that "even though I was not allowed to dance, I secretly did,"[4] she said. After everyone went to sleep, the young woman would slip silently down the stairs to Miss Ruth's dark studio. There was a tremendous peace in the room. Martha felt at ease, away from any watchful eyes. And with night as her companion, she would dance. Boldly, fully expressing her own feelings, experimenting with the beautiful movements her body made.

These dance sessions were so exhilarating that Martha only stopped when the sun began to rise. Then she stole back up to her room. Tiredness didn't enter into the picture, for she always ful-filled her daily duties at the school. She was energized at being able to express herself in the way her body needed to.

"When the time came for me to dance I would be ready,"[5] she said. That time came unexpectedly. Martha was in the dance studio teaching the solo *Serenata Morisca*, a Moorish gypsy dance, when Ted entered the room. He said that a dancer was sick and he needed a fill-in on the upcoming tour. He surveyed the room full of student dancers. His eyes rested on Martha, and he said it was too bad that she didn't know the dance, for if she did, she could replace the other dancer.

Martha jumped up and said that she could dance *Serenata Morisca*. After all, she was teaching it! Ted didn't believe her. In answer, Martha threw on a skirt and poured her entire being into *Serenata Morisca*. She must have felt very insecure about herself because after she finished, she asked if her performance was as terrible as Ted had expected. To Martha's astonishment and delight, Ted replied, "No, that is how I always wanted it to be performed. . . . And you'll do it in San Diego."[6]

And so began Martha's career as a professional dancer. Seizing the moment, Martha learned, was of paramount importance. If she had let that opportunity slip by, she might never have seen the stage.

What happened when Martha threw herself

into a dance was truly magical. Her moves were so powerful, so unique, and so riveting that she was like lightning, electrifying all those who saw her. Martha knew that she had a tremendous energy in her that even she did not fully understand. When she overheard a visitor say to Ted Shawn that she was the best dancer the company would ever have, Martha grew so frightened that she left the room. When she danced, she was just doing something that had chosen her, she would say later.

Even Miss Ruth finally admitted that Martha "would sail onto the stage like a young tornado and vitalize the entire atmosphere."[7] Soon after her *Serenata Morisca* solo performance, Martha was on stage in Denishawn's Greek, Egyptian, Indian, and Spanish dances, performing in Miss Ruth's flowing, lyrical style. The solo in *Serenata Morisca* was not her role alone, however. She had to share it with a fellow Denishawn dancer, Doris Humphrey.

Star billing for Martha came in 1920, four years after she had first started dancing. Ted cast her in the title role of *Xochitl*, based on the studies of the ancient Mayan Indian culture. *Xochitl* depicted the most beautiful Mayan maiden in the kingdom and her fight against the evil advances of the emperor, who was played by Ted.

Martha starring in Xochitl

To prepare for the exciting lead part, Martha imagined how it would feel and how she would struggle if she were violently attacked. "I wanted to be a wild, beautiful creature, maybe of another world—but very, very wild,"[8] she said. During rehearsals, Ted had not been rough in the violent scene. So during the first performance, Martha was surprised when he threw her down so hard that she actually blacked out for a few seconds. In response, Martha took an unchoreographed bite out of his arm. She later speculated that it was about this time she got the reputation of having a temper.

Ted noted that he went through the dance tour bruised and said that it felt like he was fighting with a wildcat. This was precisely the effect Martha was trying to achieve. She had become the Indian maiden fighting for her life.

Dance was Martha's life, and she expected others to take it just as seriously. This became clear to her fellow performers when, while on tour, a Denishawn dancer came to the dressing room drunk. She put her wig on backward and was joking around. Martha got so mad that she yanked a telephone out of the wall and threw it at the woman's head! Dance was what Martha loved most in the world. If she had responded by making fun of it, like the other dancer had, she would

have been saying that she didn't care about dance.

What she was becoming was a star, and critics were singling her out for excellent reviews. But she was still very humble about her work, as evidenced in an interview with the *Santa Barbara News:* "So far the only value of my work—if it has art value—is absolute sincerity," Martha said. "I would not do anything I could not feel. A dance must dominate me completely, until I lose sense of anything else. Later, what I do may be called art, but not yet."[9]

Even John Murray Anderson, a producer of the *Greenwich Village Follies,* one of America's most popular musical-dance shows, took note of Martha's performance. When Anderson traveled to California, he came to Denishawn just to see Martha dance.

Martha was not only developing artistically, she was also learning how to manage a company. When Ted was not on tour with the company, Martha supervised the other dancers and was in charge of the payroll. It was easy for her, sort of like keeping track of her little sisters. Her youngest sister, Geordie, had followed her to Denishawn and was now a company member. And Martha's earnings by now were enough to support her mother and Lizzie.

On tour, Denishawn had a few unpleasant encounters because they were performers. Once, while they were on a train to their next concert appearance, the conductor called the dancers thieves, and tried to kick them off the train. With all the dignity she could muster, Martha convinced him otherwise, and they continued on with no further problems.

From Denishawn, Martha also learned what not to do. Miss Ruth sometimes relied on improvisation, or making things up as she went along. In one dance, Miss Ruth had not fully developed the entire choreography. When she got to the vague part, Miss Ruth kept gliding around the stage, ending up near the piano player. "How much longer [is the performance], Louis?" she whispered.

"Once more around the stage, Miss Ruth," said Louis. And Ted used to say, "When in doubt, whirl."[10]

Martha saw that it was best to have everything fully developed beforehand, for improvisation failed as often as it succeeded. She was just not willing to take that chance in her own choreography.

The pianist touring with Martha and the other dancers was Louis Horst, the same man who had witnessed Martha's Denishawn audition in

1916. By now, he and Martha had spent so much time together that they were close friends. His lightheartedness and humor complemented Martha's seriousness. The two read books and discussed philosophers, but they mostly talked of dance and music. Louis was certain that Martha was going to do great things in the field of dance.

Martha herself grew so confident that she even dared to stand up to Miss Ruth. The company was on an exhausting tour across the United States, and instead of letting dancers rest after performances, Miss Ruth had them sewing costumes. Miss Ruth's costumes were almost always elaborately designed and, depending on the dance, full of lace, beads, feathers, sequins, embroidery, or bells. Miss Ruth was forever improving their look. The company couldn't afford to hire someone to do this job, so the dancers had to be seamstresses as well. Martha, as a lead dancer, must have gotten fed up with sewing, for she said, "Miss Ruth, either I am to be a dancer or a seamstress. I cannot be both."[11]

Martha was ready to accept whatever answer Miss Ruth gave, even if Miss Ruth kicked her out of the company. The truth was that Martha was growing tired of performing someone else's choreography, especially the lush, highly mannered, graceful Denishawn style of dance. She wanted to dance the way she felt, in a style from her own self, that represented who she was. However, Miss Ruth didn't kick Martha out of the company but said she didn't have to sew anymore for Denishawn. Later, though, all that experience with the needle and thread would come in handy when Martha began sewing costumes for her own dance company.

Soon after Martha took this stand against sewing, in the spring of 1922, a powerful theatrical agent named Daniel Mayer sponsored the company, along with several other acts, on a tour to London. Denishawn dancers didn't appear at serious theaters, though. Their fellow performers gave the entire show a carnival atmosphere: A pigeon act went on before them, and another animal act followed them.

After the first performance, Martha rushed out to get a newspaper to read the reviews. Her distinctive style was once again highly praised. Miss Ruth, though, got poor reviews. Martha hid the newspaper clippings and did not share her joy with anyone. She was afraid that if Miss Ruth saw the reviews she would kick her out of the company. It was heartbreaking for Martha to hear her mentor crying herself to sleep in the next room because of her poor reception.

Martha must have realized that she was out-distancing her revered teacher. She had learned all she could from Miss Ruth. She needed to explore her tremendous talent further, but she would have to do that by herself.

The time for Martha to start on her own came earlier than she expected. It was just before Denishawn was to tour the Far East. As a company star, Martha was sure she would go and was very excited about the trip. But when the list of Denishawn dancers chosen to go was posted, the only Graham noted was Geordie. Martha was too dark, too Oriental-looking, Miss Ruth explained, and the people of the Far East would not find anything exotic about her.

Martha naturally was very disappointed. All she wanted to do was dance, but she also had to support herself and her mother. Martha remembered Mr. Anderson, the *Greenwich Village Follies* owner who had liked her style of dance. She contacted him. Before she even had a chance to ask, he invited her to join the *Follies* starting on September 20, 1923.

Only after Martha signed the *Follies* contract did she see her first musical dance revue. Years later, she said, "I sat in the balcony and I cried all the way through, thinking, 'What have I let myself in for?' It was very different."[12]

Different because the performers did very basic dance steps, unlike the complicated dances Martha was used to, and the scanty costumes were intended to reveal the body. The *Follies* were part of an entertainment called vaudeville, which consisted of humorous skits, dances, songs, and animal acts. Vaudeville reached its peak of popularity in the 1920s, which were known as the Roaring Twenties. This decade was a provocative time.

However, Martha was interested in experimenting in movement and choreographing her own dances, something she could not do at the *Follies*. Luckily, she was given solos that were more artistic but that also set her apart from the other dancers. Many were jealous of her outstanding talent. It was a lonely time for Martha.

However, it was not without its moments. In Boston the dancers were reviewed by the police—before they even performed. At that time in the city, dancers were not allowed to appear in costumes that did not cover their bodies in what the police considered an adequate manner. One night, after a policeman told one of the dancers to put more clothes on, she pointed to Martha and asked, "Hey, what about her?"

Martha had less on than anyone else, but all the policeman said was, "No, she's all right. She's art."[13]

What exactly did he mean by that remark? What was the difference between Martha and the other women? Martha had one goal, to move the audience by her dance, to inspire them. She wasn't trying to convey this by the scantiness of her costume, and even outside of the performance her dignity was apparent. The policeman understood this.

Later, when the management told Martha to wear a costume for the sole purpose of showing off her body, she refused. The management tried to force her by cutting her solo out of the show. It didn't take into account Martha's popularity with the public, though. Ticket sales dropped so dramatically that the management had to give her back her solo.

Martha's ambition didn't end with becoming a *Follies* star. In fact she was becoming increasingly frustrated at not being able to develop her own dances. In 1925, she found a way out of the *Follies* by securing positions teaching dance at John Murray Anderson's Anderson-Milton School in Manhattan and at the Eastman School of Music in Rochester, New York. She was also reunited with her friend Louis Horst, who had left Denishawn and was teaching in New York. Even though she was giving up fame and fortune—perhaps forever—Martha didn't care. Finally she was free to begin developing her own style of dance.

Chapter / Three

Discovering the Dance

The instant Martha stepped inside the Eastman School of Music's dance studio, the students knew that their new teacher was going to take them places they'd never been before. And she gave them the message without saying a single word. How?

Simply, by her appearance. She was wearing a red silk Japanese kimono with slits up the sides of both legs. She wore full theatrical makeup, and her long dark hair was pulled back in a high ponytail. Silently, she walked toward the center of the studio with a dignity and gravity that made it seem like she was marching toward a throne.

Then she simply sat down cross-legged on the studio floor and directed her students to do the same.

The students were used to their former teacher's conservative dress, proper manner, and adherence to known dance steps. With few exceptions, all dance classes in America were like that. No one wore kimonos, and the closest thing to leotards were "fleshings," long-sleeved, skintight garments that students made for themselves. And no teacher started out the class with the students on the floor.

The Eastman students were astounded. They paid attention to what Martha said as they never had before in their lives. And what they experienced would change their lives.

In the beginning, Martha taught the Denishawn style of dancing she knew so well. Then Ted Shawn informed Martha that to teach the technique, she would have to pay Denishawn $500, an impossible sum to raise considering Martha's lack of finances. So thanks to what seemed to be a bad stroke of luck, the Graham Technique of modern dance was born.

It didn't happen overnight but took several years, for Martha was creating her own dance movements. She had no road map, no one to tell her how to do it. "I never set out to create a technique. I started . . . to find what the body could do, and what would give me satisfaction—emotionally, dramatically, and bodily. But I did not ever dream of establishing a technique,"[1] she said later. The studio became her laboratory. The experiments with her students became the cornerstone of the system of movement known as the Graham Technique.

Exploring uncharted territory was a little frightening at times. But Martha's excitement and her belief in what she was doing more than made up for her fear. She worked with passion, enthusiasm, and an absolute sincerity that was contagious.

Despite her overfull schedule, Martha was up each day by 6:00 A.M. and sitting on the floor of her apartment, breathing. Just breathing, for hours. Her technique was based on this essential, most elementary component of life. She began to develop movement in harmony with the rhythm of the breath.

With as much attention as she had used observing people as a child, Martha tracked what happened to the body when a person breathed. In the simple act of inhaling, the stomach expanded, followed by the lungs, and the spine straightened. Starting with the torso, one's whole body came to life. During exhalation, the body contracted. When Martha made a *sssss* sound, the stomach muscles tightened even further. She asked herself, What do the hips do? The spine?

Martha discovered how the movement of the body is affected by one's emotions. When she was happy, she observed how her body reacted, and she saw that she moved quite differently when she was angry. In Martha's dances, the meaning behind each of the body's movements was as important as the body's breathing rhythms. The slightest movement in a dance couldn't be performed without meaning. A circle around the stage had to have a reason, as did a kick or a gesture. A fall to the earth was not just a fall. Depending upon what sort of meaning it was supposed to portray, it could represent either death or a person coming to be hugged by a mother, symbolized by the earth. The emotion was conveyed by the way the dancer moved.

Later, when Martha began teaching out of her apartment, she refused to install floor-to-ceiling mirrors in the studio, another radical departure from the typical dance class. Without mirrors, it is impossible to see what you are doing—which was precisely the effect Martha wanted. Her students had to *feel* what they were doing. Classical ballet dancers, on the other hand, used the mirror to ensure their bodies were in accordance with the standard positions of ballet.

The technique of classical ballet, developed more than 350 years ago, relies on five basic positions of the arms and the feet. Each movement in every ballet starts and ends from one of these positions. The classical dancer's graceful leaps and leg extensions defy gravity and are unnatural compared to the normal way a person moves. Martha wanted her dances to be "real." She said that life "is nervous, sharp, and zigzag; it often stops in midair."[2] She tried to replicate that in her work. The result was a technique that was not pretty; it was sharp and angular.

The people who studied with Martha weren't light and delicate-looking, like classical ballet dancers. They were strong and sturdy, and they cared not about mirrors but about soaking up what she was teaching them and getting it right. Martha inspired them, and they felt every minute with her was worthwhile.

Martha's system of movements was every bit as demanding and exacting technically as classical ballet was; additionally, it allowed for the full expression of the emotions. But while Martha's experiments were very exciting to her and her stu-

Martha (center) poses with two of her early students, Evelyn Sabin (left) and Betty Macdonald (right).

dents, she was coming to realize that the Eastman School of Music did not share that excitement. The school wanted Martha to teach in the entertaining style of the *Follies* so that they could use the students in Eastman Theater performances. Martha had had enough of that kind of dance to last her for three lifetimes. How could she explain that she was teaching at a school that represented the opposite of her beliefs about dance?

She couldn't. As she entered the Eastman office to sign a contract for another teaching year, she realized she was ruining herself just for the money. Still she picked up the pen and forced her hand to start signing the contract.

She got as far as the letter M and then set the pen down. "I cannot do this,"[3] she said, and quit on the spot. Finally she was going to dance the way her spirit told her to. Martha decided she would never do anything only for money. She vowed to build her own company and perform her own works.

Martha's ambitions didn't allow her to waste a minute. In 1926, she made plans to give a debut dance concert. Other choreographers of "new" dance were doing the same in Sunday-night concerts. Since the performers had very little money, they would usually give shows from their own studios. Martha, however, chose Broadway for her debut as choreographer.

Broadway is an avenue in New York upon which the theatrical world is centered. In Martha's day, most performers who played on Broadway were already famous and sponsored by a management company. Martha was neither. The fact that she was a woman in a man's world didn't help, either. None of these things daunted her. The way Martha saw it, she might only have one chance to show her work. She would go all the way with her one shot by performing in a Broadway theater to be judged by the most influential people in the artistic world.

She knew that Mr. Green, a manager of the *Greenwich Village Follies*, owned the 48th Street Theater on Broadway. She swallowed her pride and asked him for the use of his theater for one night. Mr. Green surveyed the woman in front of him. Although at five feet two inches she was petite, her attitude and ambition were anything but tiny. She was daring to take on the giants in the theatrical arts field. She impressed Green so much that he agreed to let her use the theater on one condition: If she failed, she had to return to the *Follies* for one year.

Martha agreed. She didn't tell Green that she

didn't even have the money to pay for the theater's lighting expenses, not to mention money for advertising, costumes, tickets, the dancers, or the accompanist. She had to perform, and somehow she would. Martha turned to her friend Frances Steloff, who owned the Gotham Book Mart, for help. She asked Frances to lend her the money for the concert. Frances had never seen Martha dance. Yet she was so impressed by Martha's demeanor, sincerity, and obvious certainty in her work that she agreed to lend the sum needed, even though she didn't have it herself. Agnes de Mille, one of Martha's friends and a fellow choreographer, said that Frances pawned her jade necklace to raise the money Martha needed.

Martha had already chosen three women from her Eastman classes—Evelyn Sabin, Thelma Biracree, and Betty Macdonald—to perform with her. Louis, naturally, was Martha's accompanist. This performance was the start of a 22-year collaboration between Martha and Louis. Much of that time, Louis was Martha's musical director and editor as well as her strongest supporter.

Louis never accepted any dance movement that did not make sense or that he didn't think was good enough. He questioned Martha until she convinced him or changed the movement for the better. Sometimes, Martha lost her temper with Louis's criticism, yet he stood his ground. He simply wanted to inspire her to reach her ultimate capabilities. She sometimes said that Louis was "killing her soul," but he was so tough because he knew she was a genius.

During their collaboration together, Martha went through unavoidable periods of being lost. She would suffer over not knowing exactly which direction to choose, and she would become less productive. Then Louis would come to her studio and try to rouse her enthusiasm again. Sometimes she said, "Oh, Louis. Play me the 'Maple Leaf Rag,' "[4] by Scott Joplin. The music was so joyous and lighthearted that more often than not it helped Martha get over her artistic block.

Sometimes, though, nothing worked and Martha would grow so upset that she would threaten to stop dancing. Louis would yell right back that she should get that thought out of her mind and get back to work, and then he would leave. After a few hours, he would return, asking her what she had done. Sure enough, she would demonstrate the barest outlines of the dance that had been stuck inside her. Theirs was a highly impassioned collaboration, and Louis can be considered as much of a pioneer of modern dance as Martha was.

Louis also understood the innovative way Martha wanted to use music in the dance. Before Martha began choreographing, most dances were to be performed to the scores of classical composers, with full orchestras. The dance decorated the music, rather than being art in its own right. In Martha's dances, the purpose of music was to accent the movement. She would use only brass, woodwinds, and percussion instruments rather than strings, which she thought conveyed too romantic a feeling. The sounds of Martha's scores were bold and sharp, which suited the strong, powerful moves of her dances.

Martha and Louis probably had some heated debate as she prepared for her Broadway debut. With only one week until showtime, her three dancers traveled into New York City for final rehearsals. They worked so intensively that Martha had to be reminded to take a break for eating and sleeping, and then only a minimal one. Just before the performance, the three dancers presented Martha with a necklace that said, "To Martha with love." She decided to wear it as part of her costume. No doubt it would give her good luck, and despite her bravery, Martha was nervous about the concert, especially because it was on Broadway.

Finally, performance day, April 18, 1926, arrived. Martha was at the theater hours early. She kept peeking from behind the curtain. The theater was filling up—and so was her stomach, with butterflies.

No one had the slightest idea of her anxiety when she appeared onstage in bare feet. The program consisted of 18 short pieces, many of which were influenced by Denishawn. But then Martha began revealing her own experiments in movement, so full of emotion. The power with which she moved, the style in which she danced—all of it was new. The audience was transfixed. Before the first intermission was over, everyone in that theater knew something special was happening in the dance world. The mystery and the magic of the dance were present.

During the second intermission, Mr. Green, the theater owner, came backstage and told Martha she had made it! Martha's gamble had paid off. At the end of the show, a woman came backstage and said the performance was dreadful; how long would she keep doing it? Martha diplomatically replied, "As long as I've got an audience."[5] And this time, she had enough of an audience to repay Frances.

Martha in her first independent dance concert, on
April 18, 1926

The two opposite opinions about Martha's performance characterized reaction about her work for her entire career. People either loved it or hated it. Martha had this to say on the subject: "I'd rather an audience like me than dislike me, but I'd rather they disliked me than be apathetic, because that is the kiss of death. I know because I have had both."[6]

From 1926 to 1930, Martha would go on to create 64 dances. Every one of them challenged the way the world looked at dance. And in part due to the furor surrounding the phenomenon known as Martha Graham, the young artist became extremely famous.

Chapter / Four

Revolt!

The 1920s were a time of great change in America and the rest of the world. America had become a major economic power in the world. Machines played an increasingly important role in people's lives as more products were being mass-produced in factories. Scientists such as Albert Einstein were making groundbreaking discoveries in their fields. Psychologists such as Carl Gustav Jung and Sigmund Freud were developing new ways to study the inner workings of the mind, which affected the way people thought about themselves.

American women had finally won the right to vote in 1920. Many people admired and tried to imitate the style of the stars they saw in the movies. Cars were overtaking horse-drawn carriages as the major source of transport. The Roaring Twenties style of life swept across the country as more Americans became affluent.

For the rest of the world, the twenties were also a time of great turmoil. Europe was recovering from the devastation of World War I, which had taken millions of lives. The people of many European countries were suffering because of national economic problems. Some began supporting dictators, thinking this would solve their unhappiness.

In the arts, painters, actors, musicians, and writers responded to the changes and turmoil through their work. They developed new forms of expression called modern art. Martha represented the modernist movement in her dance. Her viewpoint became very clear in the dance *Revolt*. It premiered October 16, 1927, at her second concert.

Revolt means to "vigorously express one's disagreement." Everyone, at one time or another, has desired to do so. Martha took that desire and created an outlet with which everyone could identify.

What was *Revolt* protesting against? Against people's cruelty to one another? Against the attention people were giving to machines instead of

Martha in Revolt

their souls? Against the hurt a child feels when confronted by such a reality? Against the pain an artist experiences when attempting only to share her sensitivity in such a cold world and being rejected? Many people interpreted *Revolt* as all of these things combined.

In the dance, Martha revolted against the graceful, airy curves of Denishawn. Sharp, staccato movements with a dissonant musical score characterized the dance. Her jumps were powerful jolts. Her walks were heavy staggers. Her runs were wild. She replaced the ornate costumes of Denishawn with a simple, unadorned sleeveless dress. *Revolt* was a revolution!

Martha was forging new ground in the dance world in that she was portraying realistic human desires as well as current social issues. She called her style of dance contemporary because it dealt with current issues. *Immigrant*, which premiered on April 22, 1928, focuses on the plight of the many people coming to America during that time. In their native countries, these people had heard that the streets of America were "paved with gold," and so the immigrants expected to become rich. What they found, however, was work that paid almost nothing—in very poor conditions. Martha's dance conveyed how this dashing of their dreams made them feel.

Martha became more popular, a fact that did not sit well with her rival and former Denishawner Doris Humphrey. She and Martha now competed for the number-one spot in the contemporary dance world. Their competition, however, did not stop them from attending each other's concerts to see what the other was up to.

Both Martha's and Doris's ambitions were threatened when the Roaring Twenties and America's explosive economic growth came to a grinding halt in 1929. The country had fallen into a deep depression. Martha herself was so poor at this time that she sometimes had to borrow money from Louis to get through the day. Fifty cents was enough for the subway, a cup of coffee, and a roll.

Lack of money, however, can never stop a true artist from expressing art. If an artist feels with all his or her being that something inside must be said because the world in some way will be enlightened, the artist will find a way to not let that vision die. Martha was one of those artists.

Many businesses across the country during the Great Depression were going bankrupt. And there were plenty of people in New York who couldn't find jobs and didn't have money to pay their rent. But there were still enough people to save Martha from going bankrupt. They saved their pennies and took Martha's classes. And they attended her concerts.

The critics were still divided about Martha's artistic merit. Nonetheless, they were compelled to attend every one of her concerts. Throughout the early thirties, they wrote that she baffled and perplexed almost as many as she inspired. One critic called her style of dance "modern duncing." Another said he was afraid to attend her performances because she might give birth to a cube.

Undaunted, Martha kept teaching and refining her technique. More students signed up for her classes, and she was also teaching at the Neighborhood Playhouse, a dramatic arts school dedicated to helping an individual find his or her talents and the ideal way for expressing them. Louis accompanied her on piano at classes and rehearsals and also taught dance composition.

Martha would tell her students that one of them was doomed to be a dancer, without singling out any one in particular. Each hoped to be the lucky one so "doomed." Martha saw enough talent in her students that she decided to expand her all-female concert trio of dancers. Those students chosen thought that Martha held the key to life itself. She fascinated them with her boldness and independence, and her curiosity about the world was contagious. The students read books by important philosophers, visited museums, and endlessly discussed what Martha meant by doing this movement instead of that one. They came to know themselves better than they had before.

Working with Martha didn't pay their rent. Yet their lives revolved around her work. They studied with her in the early mornings. Around 8:00 A.M., they left to work at their jobs. Afterward, no matter how tired they were, they returned to Martha's studio to perform some more work.

They knew that they would earn only ten dollars a concert, with no more than two concerts a year, but it didn't matter. The dancers' fatigue was instantly replaced with energy as soon as Martha began demonstrating the moves she wanted them to perform. They knew they were in the presence of a genius who was changing the way people looked at dance. Agnes de Mille, Martha's good friend and a fellow choreographer, wrote that Martha's early dance groups "had the fervor of a medieval religious cult and the physical energy of the ancient Greek athletes, who were quite willing to die in order to obtain the Marathon laurels."[1]

Since she had no money to purchase costumes, Martha designed them. The dancers would sit in a circle on the studio floor sewing, just like Martha had done at Denishawn. To save money, several dancers shared apartments. Anna Sokolow, one of the smallest, was said to have slept in a laundry bag. Martha "brought out a creativity in us that we didn't know we had,"[2] Anna said. She would later become an internationally acclaimed choreographer.

While Martha couldn't give her dancers more money, she and Louis helped them by securing them scholarships at the Neighborhood Playhouse, giving free private lessons, and finding them jobs. She made sure they were clothed and fed and had shelter. Since the dancers spent so much time together, they celebrated birthdays and holidays together as family. Martha often brought her two dachshunds, Allah and Madel, to the studio. The dogs were the only ones who didn't have aching muscles at the end of a long day of rehearsals.

When Martha got a wave of inspiration, she'd keep the dancers in the studio rehearsing all night long. The dance *Heretic* was created in just such a manner. It premiered on April 14, 1929, and was one of the first dances Martha performed with her larger concert group. A heretic is a person who is condemned for not following the traditional norms of society. During the Spanish Inquisition, people were burned at the stake for being heretics. In *Heretic*, Martha explored how society reacts to outsiders and how it feels to be one. She drew on her own experience to create the dance. "I felt at the time that I was a heretic. I was outside the realm of women. I did not dance the way people danced. . . . I used the floor. I used the flexed foot. I showed effort. My foot was bare. In many ways I showed onstage what most people came to the theatre to avoid,"[3] Martha wrote in her autobiography.

In *Heretic*, Martha appeared onstage dressed in white. Two columns of women in long dark dresses surrounded her, marching menacingly toward her. She made pleading gestures for acceptance, to no avail. She tried to escape, but they closed the ranks of their columns and she fell to the ground. She stood up again, her white dress radiating light in the darkness. "Please," her body seemed to plead, "just let me live, that's all I am trying to do." Even these delicate gestures were full of power. Yet the "soldiers" beat her down again. In the end, Martha collapsed. The heretic had been punished. In reality, however, Martha's star continued to rise.

In Heretic, Martha *explored what it feels like to be an outcast.*

Inspiration for each dance did not often come as easily as it did with *Heretic*. And as a heretic, Martha didn't have anyone to turn to for advice. Even Louis couldn't tell her how to dance. To relieve tensions, she visited the Central Park Zoo. She observed the movements of the lions for hours, trying to extend her comprehension of the movement of the body, until sometimes, she said, the zookeeper *and* the lions viewed her suspiciously.

By 1930, Martha's lack of finances grew severe. She had to form a sort of partnership with several of her rivals—Doris Humphrey, Charles Weidman, and Helen Tamaris—to stage joint performances under the name the Modern Dance Repertory. The partners pooled their money to rent concert halls and to advertise.

Martha premiered *Lamentation* on January 8, 1930, on the Repertory program. Martha did the unthinkable in this dance: She didn't take even one step. She sat on a bench, dressed in a long tube of fabric stretched over her head like a hood. Her legs were spread, her feet clutched at the ground, and she writhed and rocked, giving the appearance of a woman in agony. Martha was revealing what grief looks like on the inside of the soul.

One woman was so moved that she started crying. Martha later learned that the woman had seen her son killed in a car accident and had been unable to cry. "I realized that grief was a dignified and valid emotion and that I could yield to it without shame," said the woman.[4] Martha knew from experience that pain is part of life.

The *New York Times* dance critic John Martin wrote, "She does the unforgivable thing for a dancer to do—she makes you think. . . . Frequently the vividness and intensity . . . strike like a blow. . . . Miss Graham deals more and more in essences. . . . She is a constant surprise."[5] He

Martha gave new meaning to the word dance *in* Lamentation, *in which she took not a single step.*

wasn't the only one praising her. Martha was winning over almost all the critics who earlier had been against her.

It came as no surprise to the dance world when Martha was approached by the world-famous conductor and composer Leopold Stokowski, who was working with the Philadelphia Orchestra. He was experimenting in music as Martha was in dance. Now he wanted to revive one of the first modern dances ever performed, *The Rite of Spring*.

Martha would be the dancer, and Léonide Massine of the famous Ballets Russes, a classical ballet company, would reconstruct the choreography. The two were exact opposites in their approach to dance. When Léonide visited Martha's very bare apartment to discuss the possibility of working together, the two had little to say. She knew that it would be difficult, but she took that challenge and put up with Massine's whispering during rehearsals that she should quit.

Martha wasn't about to be intimidated by anyone. She knew that to be chosen for the project was a great honor. She would become better known because of the wide publicity the performance would receive and the historic importance of the dance itself. When *The Rite of Spring* was first performed in 1913 in Paris, it caused a near riot in the theater. One man who had applauded the show had been hit over the head with an umbrella by a woman who did not share his enthusiasm.

Nothing like that happened in Martha's performance, which was very successful despite the sparks that had flown between her and Massine in rehearsals. And Martha's fame grew.

Chapter / Five

Making History

During the summers, Martha and Louis traveled to the desert of the Southwest and then to see
Martha's mother in California. They loved these
breaks from their hectic lives in New York, especially because they got to visit the pueblos of
Native Americans. Most of the time, the native
peoples welcomed Martha and Louis to watch
their ceremonial dances. Martha was drawn by the
simplicity, sincerity, rhythm, and reverence in the
dances. They were a rich source of inspiration for
her own work. Perhaps the simple Native
Americans dances inspired Martha to introduce
herself to one of her new classes by saying,
"Putting on shoes is like wearing gloves to keep
you away from the filthy earth!"[1]

In one instance, just after arriving in Gallup,

New Mexico, from New York, Martha and Louis heard about a rain dance at a Zuni pueblo. The public was not invited, and they were warned not to attend. They went anyway, ignoring the rumor that the Zuni had once caused a plane to fall when it flew over their reservation against their wishes.

Very early on in the rain dance, it began raining hard. The Zuni dancers yelled even louder for Martha and Louis to leave. They did, but Louis contracted pneumonia as a result of being out in the rain so long. Martha spent the rest of the summer nursing Louis back to health.

In the summer of 1931, Martha was in Seattle, teaching at the Cornish School as a guest artist. The dancers had heard of her recent success in the historic revival of *The Rite of Spring*, but she scarcely mentioned that performance. Instead she said that they had a lot of work to do, so they had better get busy.

The dancers soon learned just how serious she was. By the day's end, their feet were so sore that they could hardly walk. Dorothy Bird, one of the students, said, "Everybody was hypnotized, absolutely magnetized by Martha. It was like a mass falling in love, but much, much more. . . . She opened our eyes to the arts. I was on fire."[2]

Studying with Martha was fun, too. Dorothy

said, "With Martha, you did all the things you love."[3] This included running, skipping, breathing, standing, laughing, crying, and jumping—important things that children do but adults sometimes seem to forget about. Then Martha would experiment with segmenting, or cutting off those moves. For example, she would have the dancers run around in a circle. Then she would have them start the circle but stop halfway around, then cut it off at a quarter way around, and so on. She was stripping movement down to its very essence.

Martha told stories to get the students to understand what she wanted them to do. The stories made sense both for dance and for life. As a result, her teaching gave the dancers a wider perspective from which to view the world. When Martha was teaching the class to swing the arms and project emotion, she said that the students were trying to break a rock. Not any old rock, but the sturdiest of rocks, such as the Rock of Gibraltar or the brick walls of Jericho. She knew that putting the image of something as extreme as the Rock of Gibraltar in their minds would force her students to go all out with their movement. And she was right. Dorothy and the other students were so inspired that they went out at dawn to a park to find the biggest rock and started pounding away. "We didn't break it, but we projected,"[4] Dorothy concluded.

"For each thing she had a whole way of catching your imagination. . . . She had us shouting 'No!' then sobbing and hiding our grief," said Dorothy.

"Then she told us that for dessert we would do laughter. 'The Chinese think laughter is a very healthy thing,' [Martha] said. 'But we will not do it again. You have it in your muscular memory now. You will put it in your muscles—if it's in your rib cage, now you can put it in your knees—so it's a secret. The audience will be terribly intrigued,'" Dorothy remembered Martha telling the dancers.[5]

Within the year, Dorothy made her way to New York with only twenty dollars to study with Martha. Bonnie Bird, another student in that class (not related to Dorothy), followed and joined the company in 1933.

Martha challenged her new dancers in more ways than one. Jean Erdman, who joined the company in 1938, learned almost instantly that Martha demanded—and got—the impossible from her dancers. "When I was invited to join the company, upon arrival at the studio, I found that I had to learn four dances in ten days prior to my first performance in Boston," said Jean. "The only thing I remember about the performance is that . . . when I could stop jumping and breathe, I saw stars—the only time in my life that I saw stars from sheer exhaustion!"[6]

Martha instilled in her dancers the same drive and discipline that she herself had. The actual teaching was only part of how she did it; her attitude also played a part. To her, dance "cost no less than everything." It was life itself, to be approached with reverence and respect. "Where a dancer stands ready," Martha often said, "that spot is holy ground."

In her biography of Martha, Agnes de Mille wrote, "Conversations with Martha were like someone running around the house opening windows. There seemed to be one intent: air."[7]

Many who danced with Martha—especially Anna Sokolow, May O'Donnell, and Jean Erdman—became the foot soldiers of modern dance. After they left Martha's group, they fanned out across the United States, establishing their own companies or modern-dance schools.

Many actors that Martha taught at the Neighborhood Playhouse also went on to become stars in theater and film, including Bette Davis, Joanne Woodward, and Gregory Peck. She cowed the men who were suspicious of her approach by

saying that she was going to at least teach them
how to walk like men. Once, when the actors
didn't stop talking after she arrived at a class, she
just stood ramrod straight without saying a word
or even looking at them. "I sensed they were set-
tling down and staring at me," said Martha. Then
she said, "There are tears rolling down inside my
cheeks." The image so surprised the students that
they instantly became quiet. "They all wanted
that kind of power and drama," said Martha.[8]

Years later, in another acting class, Martha
was lecturing on how everything the performer
does must appear effortless. As she spoke, she
raised her leg and extended it straight out from
the side of her hip without looking at it. She kept
it there through the entire lecture, as if to demonstrate the point. When she finished, she glanced
at her leg as if to say, "It's all right now, you can
lower yourself back to the floor." Martha made the
actors realize how important every single move
can be.

"I worshipped her," said legendary film siren
Bette Davis. "She was all tension. . . . She would,
with a single thrust of her weight, convey anguish.
Then . . . she became all joy. . . . There was no end
once the body was disciplined. What at first
seemed 'grotesque to the eye' developed into a

beautiful release for both dancer and beholder."[9]

As a teacher, Louis was just as inspiring and as much of a taskmaster as Martha. And woe to the dancer who didn't come prepared to his dance composition class at the Neighborhood Playhouse. At the piano in Martha's classes and rehearsals, Louis often kept his eyes half closed, as if he were sleeping. But the dancers learned that appearances were very deceiving, especially in Louis's case. From a seeming dream, he would suddenly tell Martha that a student had dropped her leg.

The "dance policeman" was also an invaluable easer of tensions. This was especially important before performance times, when Martha's and the dancers' nerves were running high. As is typical of most performers, they would grow increasingly anxious as the date of a concert came near. Martha's nervousness displayed itself in alarming ways. One thing she did was to redesign costumes right before a concert, just as Miss Ruth used to do.

She did just this only 48 hours before the premiere of *Primitive Mysteries*. At the premiere, on February 2, 1931, Anna Sokolow still hadn't finished her dress, and she had to appear onstage with her costume safety-pinned together.

Primitive Mysteries, with a musical score by Louis, reenacts a ceremony in honor of the Virgin

Louis Horst, Martha's composer and collaborator for many years

Mary, played by Martha. There are three parts to the dance. The first, "Hymn of the Virgin," glorifies through Mary the positive impact that a faithful, selfless, loving, and innocent woman can have on people. The second part, "Crucifixus," has Mary and the chorus witness the agony of Jesus Christ being crucified on the cross. The third,

"Hosanna," celebrates the resurrection of Jesus Christ and emphasizes hope, joy, and victory of the spirit over death.

Martha drew her inspiration for the dance from Christian-influenced ceremonial rituals of the southwestern Native Americans and from her own childhood experience of visiting Catholic churches. *Primitive Mysteries* was so important to her that she had been working on it for a year. During that time the dancers had often come to the studio for rehearsals to find her sitting on the floor. She wouldn't even look up to say hello, for she didn't want to break her concentration. Eventually, she would think through the moves in her mind and would begin working them out on herself and her dancers.

She made the dancers repeat the moves in *Primitive Mysteries* with slight variations, hour after hour, sometimes for weeks. What decided whether a movement was ready to be used in a dance was not time, but whether it was perfect according to Martha's vision. Just the opening walk for *Primitive Mysteries* took months to get right. The dancers had to walk onto the stage without music. To perform in sync is extremely difficult in any case. It was more so in this particular dance, because the only signals the dancers had

Martha in the role of the Virgin Mary in Primitive Mysteries

to guide their moves were one another's breaths.

The group experienced its own transformation during rehearsals. One of the dancers, Gertrude Shurr, said, "Martha really gave us a marvelous quietness that permeated the whole group. Everyone felt it, this belief in oneness . . . . When she put out her hand to bless, when she touched you, when she was performing, it was not Martha, it was the *other*."[10]

Although this dance meant more to Martha than any other, the group had only one chance to rehearse in the theater—on the day of the concert. She couldn't afford to rent the theater even one more day. Understandably, this made Martha more anxious than usual. Just before midnight, Martha and her group entered the theater to rehearse, "but the dance was not working,"[11] said Martha. When she moved backwards to step on a platform formed by the thighs of one of the dancers, Martha lost her balance and her temper. "Go home!" she shouted at her dancers, and then she walked off the stage. She felt sure the dance would fail.

The exhausted dancers did not move. They waited, as Louis went after Martha. No one wanted this important work to fail. Somehow, Louis was able to convince Martha to finish the rehearsal. Afterward, the dancers left to snatch a few hours of sleep. They returned at 9:00 A.M. to the theater to rehearse until just one hour before curtain call.

Martha probably did not sleep at all. Everyone was so keyed up, though, that they probably didn't miss the sleep. By now, Martha was so nervous that she couldn't even talk. That evening, when Martha and her group performed *Primitive Mysteries*, they made history.

The audience rose and clapped wildly. The company received 23 curtain calls! "For those short minutes during which Martha celebrated her ritual, Christ was crucified and the Virgin assumpted into heaven," wrote Agnes de Mille. In fact, Martha had merged dance with the most holy event of the Christian religion. "Every man and woman in the house watching approached divine awareness," wrote de Mille.[12] Martha was so overcome by the audience's reaction that, just as before the premiere, she couldn't speak.

New Republic dance critic Stark Young, who had written negative reviews of Martha's work, wrote, "I can say it is one of the few things I have ever seen in dancing where the idea, its origin, the source from which it grew, the development of its excitement and sanctity, give me a sense of baffled awe and surprise, the sense of wonder and defeat in its beautiful presence."[13]

John Martin of *The New York Times* wrote, "Here is a composition which must be ranked among the choreographic masterpieces of the modern dance movement. . . . She has already touched the borderland of that mystic territory where greatness dwells."[14]

Chapter / Six

Beyond the Frontier

The taste of success was sweet to Martha, and in 1932 she proudly stepped up to the podium to receive a Guggenheim fellowship honoring her contributions as an artist. It was the first Guggenheim fellowship ever awarded to a dancer and the first of dozens of awards Martha would eventually receive for her artistic genius.

From February through November 1932, Martha and her group gave concerts that took them from Tallahassee, Florida, to Boston, Massachusetts and from Richmond, Virginia, to Ann Arbor, Michigan. The American people filled auditoriums to see the dancers. Sometimes the audience reactions were surprising. For instance, after one performance, a football coach asked Martha about the secret signals that she gave the performers in order to get them to move in unison.

The tours cost a small fortune. Martha had huge debts, despite her own cost-saving procedures, including spending only one dollar per costume. Though she was always perfectly attired, it wasn't because she was buying a lot of clothes. It was because she took care to make sure the few nice dresses that she owned were always in perfect condition.

Martha knew that if she had continued in the *Follies*, she would have been able to afford hundreds of dresses by now. But she chose to discover new forms of dance instead of discovering how much money she could make. The importance of living in luxury paled in comparison with the importance of her work. Martha's wealthy friends helped her in many ways, including giving her small sums of money. She never asked them for the amounts that she truly needed, though. She felt that if someone wanted to give her a gift, it should be motivated by that person's own desire, not by being asked for help.

One of these people was Katherine Cornell, a

famous stage actress. She had seen *Primitive Mysteries* and wanted to make sure that more people saw Martha's work. She gave Martha money to have a week-long season on Broadway in 1934, the longest season an American dancer had ever had.

In summer 1934, Martha and Louis didn't head to the Southwest. Instead they piled their run-down car with luggage, managed to find space for Martha's two dachshunds and drove 194 miles north to Bennington College in Vermont. Among all the farmers in their overalls, Martha with her elegant, exotic appearance and Louis in his rumpled suit and tie looked totally out of place. But they enjoyed the odd looks that people gave them.

They were among the first teachers to work at the college's new summer dance program. Martha Hill, one of Martha's former dancers, headed the program. She chose the best modern dancers to be teachers, including Martha's rivals Hanya Holm and Doris Humphrey. The college's curricula included everything related to the art of dance: stage design, music composition, and dance criticism. Students and teachers of dance throughout the nation came to study in the new summer program. The teachers left their individual col-

Louis Horst and Martha at Bennington College in Vermont, where Martha choreographed many classic dances

leges giving lessons in tap and folk dance and returned teaching Martha's dance style of contractions and releases.

At Bennington, Martha had the luxury of developing even more dances for her repertory because the college funded all concerts and rehearsals. She had the pleasure of rehearsing her dancers on the campus lawns, and she enjoyed a wonderful view from the carriage barn that had been converted into her living quarters. The fact that she didn't have a driver's license didn't stop her from taking scenic drives. But when she drove, program director Martha Hill told the other passengers to pray. Otherwise, she said, with Martha's driving, there might never have been a future for modern dance.

One of the dances Martha developed at Bennington was *Frontier: An American Perspective of the Plains*, the first of several dances known as her American cycle. Louis composed the musical score. For the first time, Martha used set decoration. Up until then, her dances had been performed on a stark stage with a dark curtain for a backdrop—the way she had wanted. Most choreographers, however, used painted backdrops portraying realistic scenes. Martha chose the famous sculptor Isamu Noguchi to create pieces for her.

Isamu's work was abstract. His sculptures merely suggested the objects they were to portray. For example, a prop of a mirror did not contain reflective glass, only an elaborately sculpted frame. His sculptures, in some instances, actually became extensions of the dance. All his pieces worked toward suggesting the ideas that Martha wanted to convey. *Frontier* was the start of a 53-year collaboration between Isamu and Martha. "I was just her assistant with the necessary equipment, like in a hospital,"[1] Isamu humbly said.

In *Frontier*, Isamu's stage design was simple:

Two horizontal poles served as a fence. The fence represented the idea of crossing over borders into the unknown, a place of discovery. The dance opened with Martha in a simple sand-colored jumper over a white blouse. She boldly gazed out at the audience, which represented the frontier. She marched, leaped, and kicked her way joyously toward them. Suddenly she drew back as if blown by the wind of the prairie. Then she advanced forward again and again fell back. By the end, she radiated with the determination and confidence that helped our country's settlers in their quest.

True art takes on many more meanings than the one that the artist intends. Just as Martha achieved this in *Primitive Mysteries*, she achieved it with *Frontier*. When Martha raised her hand to her forehead and stared out at the unknown, some remembered themselves as teenagers on the frontier of adulthood. To others, she seemed to be a woman about to enter the frontier of marriage, a college graduate starting out in her career, or a marathon runner determined to reach the finish line.

Martha danced in that classic when she was 41 years old. Most dancers' careers are over when they are in their thirties because their bodies can no longer take the physical demands of dance. Martha, on the other hand, was wildly, joyously,

and fully exploring the possibilities of her art—
and they seemed, at the time, to be endless.

That same year, Martha received an invitation to dance at the upcoming 1936 Olympics in
Germany. An appearance for any artist at the
Olympics meant instant recognition. He or she
would be assured a financial future and an international artistic reputation. The invitation was the
opportunity of a lifetime.

Martha took one second to answer—
absolutely not. At that time the German government was one of the cruelest and most repressive
in the world. Among other atrocities, the government harassed artists and limited their freedom. It
established laws particularly against Jews, Gypsies,
and other minorities, designed to make their lives
miserable. Those who spoke out against the government would likely find themselves out of a job
and under close and uncomfortable scrutiny by the
government.

Just as Martha said there were only two kinds
of dance, good and bad, she likely thought there
were only two kinds of people, good and bad.
Certainly, she did not like anyone who tried to
limit the growth of the human spirit. To appear at
the Olympics would be against everything she
believed in.

Germany's government representative tried to get Martha to change her mind. He had no idea with whom he was dealing. When Martha said that most of her company members were Jewish, he argued that they would be treated differently from the German Jews. "And do you think I would ask them to go?"[2] Martha responded. After he said he would ask another American dance company instead, Martha informed him she would spread the word across America that Germany had had to settle for second best.

The German official gave up trying to black-mail Martha into performing and also decided it wasn't such a good idea to ask any other American dance company to appear, either. And how right Martha was to refuse. Five years later, in 1939, Germany invaded Poland, and the Second World War began. In this worldwide battle of good against evil, more than 17 million lives were lost, 6 million of them Jews. Martha later discovered that her own name was on the list of people the German government planned to execute once the United States was defeated.

Despite Martha's stand for human rights, she always said that she never discussed politics or religion. But her actions spoke louder than words. When a famous black singer, Marian Anderson, was refused admittance to the Algonquin Hotel in New York City because of her skin color, Martha called for her bags and left the hotel in protest. In response to the atrocities committed against inno-cent people during the Spanish civil war, she created *Deep Song*, a dance that portrays the tragedy and devastation that war wreaks upon the human spirit.

In 1937, another invitation from a top gov-ernment official came to her door. This time, she instantly agreed. The request was to perform at the White House for President Roosevelt and the First Lady. While the Roosevelts were familiar with Martha's style of dance, some of the presi-dent's aides were not. One kept telling Martha that she would not be allowed to appear barefoot before the president.

Her trademark was to dance barefoot—how could this individual not know? The comment was like telling the world's most famous painter at that time, Pablo Picasso, that he couldn't use a brush. Martha calmly informed the aide that she had no intention of meeting the president barefoot but that her bare feet were part of her costume and she would dance without shoes. No more questions were asked, and the performance went off without a hitch.

Performing for the president at the White House was, and is, one of the highest honors for an American artist. Martha was now recognized as one of the finest artists in the country. She returned to the White House and danced in her bare feet before seven more presidents.

Chapter / Seven

New Directions and a Nightmare

In 1936, Martha had an encounter that changed her life and her company. It happened during her summer residency at Bennington, where she attended the Ballet Caravan's debut concert. Afterward, she went backstage and singled out one young dancer for compliments. His name was Erick Hawkins. His career was just starting, and he was proud and surprised to receive praise from such an important individual. Martha's reaction to him was the subject of much speculation among other performers, for she never praised lightly.

Martha's dance style intrigued Erick, and he began to study with her. Then she did something she had never done before: She invited Erick to watch rehearsals. Martha had always conducted rehearsals in secrecy. Allowing Erick access to this confidential process gave her dancers the first inkling that this man had affected her deeply.

Martha surprised everybody again by allowing Erick to join the company—the first male in her group. She revised American Document, the dance she'd been working on, to include him and another man onstage. The second man did not dance but instead narrated the action. Martha was excited about the new direction her work was taking, especially since no modern or classical choreographer had used narration in performance before.

American Document, which premiered August 6, 1938, portrays through dance the development of America. It depicts Native Americans, the arrival of the Puritans, and the establishment of the United States. For the narration, Martha chose excerpts of famous American poems, speeches (including one by President Roosevelt), historical documents, proclamations, and sermons.

In the dance Martha arranged, 13 dancers onstage represent the first 13 states. The narrator's voice reads, "We hold these truths to be self-evident, that all men are created equal," the

Martha performing with Erick Hawkins, whom she married in 1948

famous words of the Declaration of Independence. Then the dancers burst from the line and run and leap for joy across the stage.

"When I saw those girls standing there, I trod clouds of glory,"[1] said Pearl Lang, who became one of those dancers in 1941. Pearl later took over some of Martha's solos. When she left the Graham company, Pearl established her own company and became an internationally acclaimed modern dancer and choreographer.

Nelle Fisher was one of the dancers who had so inspired Pearl. Pearl had no clue that it was Nelle's first time performing with the group. Nelle recalled how she had learned to do the pony prance for the performance rehearsals. Martha assured her she was doing fine. Then Martha hit Nelle on the backside so hard that her body went into a convulsion. "My hip came up, my arms flew up, with my head thrown back,"[2] said Nelle. Nelle's moves were now perfect for the dance. She didn't need another swat to execute the pony prance perfectly.

Meanwhile, Erick's presence as a Graham dancer was generally accepted by the critics but not so well received by many of Martha's other dancers. She sought his opinion more than theirs, and she chose him to teach rehearsals, rather than the other dancers who had been with the company much longer. Some of her dancers felt betrayed that he was playing such an important role in the company. That year, four of Martha's performers left the company.

Then Martha informed her dancers that they would be studying ballet with Erick. If Martha had said, "I am giving up my career to become a lawyer," they would not have been more surprised. The Graham dancers, in many cases, had been trained to move in a manner opposed to balletic technique. Why did Martha make this decision? Because ballet, with its well-developed exercises, has something to offer any dancer in the way of solid physical training.

Erick's presence also coincided with Martha's work taking on even more new dimensions. Her dances became more theatrical and dramatic. She started using ballet techniques to reinforce the dancers' physical strength, and she adapted some ballet movements to use in her dances. For example, she used the turnout of the legs, which enabled a performer to jump higher.

Martha never spoke of private matters with her dancers, and none of the group dared to question her on them, but it was clear that she was in love with her leading man. In Erick, Martha seemed to have found the partner she likely thought only existed in fairy tales. She may have thought there was no limit to the heights they could achieve together. Erick also began taking over some of Louis's work: He helped organize tours and secure funding, and he oversaw the physical side of the productions—the moving and setting up of the scenery. This help gave Martha more time to create dances.

And create she did—with amazing variety. *Every Soul Is a Circus*, a satirical comedy, premiered in 1939. The male dancer Merce Cunningham debuted in this dance. When he left the company in 1945, he established his own, currently one of the world's finest. By 1940, Martha had created 114 dances. Among them were two classics, *El Penitente*, which was inspired by southwestern Native American ceremonies, and *Letter to the World*, which focuses on one of the greatest American poets, Emily Dickinson.

How did Martha get her ideas? From the things that she did every day. She read literature, poetry, and the Bible. She watched people. Many times, she and Louis just stood on the street and observed the action around them. She listened to the news and watched films. In her autobiography, she wrote that she gained inspiration from "the diversity of a tree or the ripple of the sea, a bit of poetry, a sighting of a dolphin breaking the still water and moving toward me . . . anything that quickens you to the instant."[3]

Martha's works were so unique that without

original musical scores to accompany them, they simply would not have worked. But she didn't have money to hire composers, and while Louis had composed many scores for Martha, he was now very busy teaching and lecturing, as well as editing *Dance Observer*, a modern dance magazine he founded in 1933. The problem was solved when Elizabeth Sprague Coolidge, a music lover, commissioned three of the world's finest composers—Aaron Copland, Paul Hindemith, and Carlos Chávez—to create scores for three of Martha's new works. The first two dances premiered at the Library of Congress on October 30, 1944.

Aaron Copland wrote the musical score for the first work. He called it simply "Ballet for Martha." Martha named the dance *Appalachian Spring*. It became one of her most popular modern ballets, and Copland won a Pulitzer Prize for the musical score. *Appalachian Spring* depicts the marriage of a young couple who are setting out on the frontier. They seem bursting with love, full of hope for the future, as they move into their first house and farm. In the dance, it seems that everything good is possible for the couple.

Of *Appalachian Spring*, Martha said, "If you have seen spring come, the first shimmer of one of

those willow trees in the light . . . it is that
moment of new life, or promise, of awakening.
That's why the scenery for this dance is the frame-
work of the house . . . just the outline. . . . it's the
structure on which the house is built and behind
the structure is the emotion that builds the house
which is love."[4]

Paul Hindemith composed the score for the
second dance, *Herodiade*. This dance was quite a
departure from Martha's American cycle of works.
To create it, she looked into the soul of her own
self and drew out something every woman—and
man—can relate to: being terrified of growing old
and realizing that perhaps your life has not been
lived to its fullest and that you may never achieve
your dreams. Martha resolved this problem by
having the character accept her destiny; the
message is that the most important thing in life is
to love and accept yourself no matter what. The
idea for this dance struck Martha when she questioned a simple thing that we do every day
without thinking. She asked: "When you look in
the mirror, what do you see? Do you only see what
you want to see and not what is there? Sometimes
you do, sometimes you don't. . . . A mirror is an
instrument . . . to arrive at the truth."[5]

The action in the dance centers around an

aging woman staring into a mirror, not very happy at her image. Isamu created the mirror, which was the sculpture of a frame that had no glass in it. When Mr. Hindemith, not used to this kind of "scenery," asked where the mirror was, Martha replied, ". . . I'm dealing with the magic of the mind, not the actuality."[6]

Another "angel" attracted to Martha's magic of the mind was the Frenchwoman Bethsabée de Rothschild, a member of a wealthy Jewish family. During World War II, just before the Germans conquered France, the Rothschilds fled to America. Bethsabée started taking classes with Martha. While she never danced professionally, she so loved Martha's work that she began touring with the company as a helper, accepting no pay. Bethsabée freely helped Martha to commission more musical scores and to pay for dancers' salaries, costumes, and stage decor. Her funding also enabled Martha to have a one-week season each year.

Martha also signed with the biggest talent-management agent in the United States, Sol Hurok. He sponsored Martha's tours in exchange for part of the proceeds. Although he had worked with two other pioneering contemporary dancers—Isadora Duncan and Mary Wigman of

Germany—he said that Martha was the best.

All the success, though, didn't negate the challenge of living on the road. The dancers traveled by bus, often staying in a city only one or two days and then moving on to the next stop. No doubt the dancers sometimes awoke in the middle of the night wondering where they were. One-night stands were grueling. The company had to set up the stage design and lighting, check the theater's sound system, rehearse, and adjust to an unfamiliar stage. They had to mend costumes and iron them, not to mention washing their own clothes and finding places to eat. Then they'd travel to the next city and start all over again.

Plenty of other people would have taken a break from creating new dances, but not Martha. From 1943 to 1950, she created 13 new dances, several of them hailed as masterpieces. Some of those dances depicted heroines in Greek mythology. The dances' characters went on "soul adventures," as Martha's good friend Joseph Campbell, the mythologist and philosopher, said. The heroines went on adventures that portrayed universal struggles of good against evil. They had to decide which side they were on, and in the process they came to understand who they were and who they were capable of being. Martha said that she identi-

fied with these stories, she called them primal, but
not primitive, and described them as being the
landscape of a person's soul. Although the stories
take place in Greece, she explained that the myth
is universal, that the experiences are common ones
with which everyone can identify. Through watching Martha's dances, many people were given the
opportunity to reflect on their own behavior,
whether they liked it or not. For instance, the terrible things that happen when someone acts out of
hatred and jealousy were revealed in *Cave of the
Heart*. The dance shows how the ancient Greek
heroine Medea takes terrible revenge upon
others—killing her husband's second wife and her
children—for wrongs she thinks have been done to
her. As a result, she ends up alone, doomed to
relive in her mind her horrible deeds. The dance
Night Journey, which evolved from the Greek story
Oedipus Rex, depicts Queen Jocasta in the instant
she learns that something she did many years
before has caused a terrible tragedy—to herself, her
family, and her kingdom. She herself then takes
responsibility for her act in an equally tragic
manner. In Martha's hands, the dance demonstrated in part how every act a person commits has
a consequence and that eventually one must
assume responsibility for one's acts.

The strength that comes from facing one's fear and overcoming it was depicted in *Errand into the Maze*, based on the ancient story of the Minotaur. The Minotaur is a monster so wild and dangerous that he is put into a maze from which he can never find his way out. The humans who venture into the maze face two equally terrifying fates: being eaten by the Minotaur or being lost forever in the maze. The secret of the maze is then revealed in the dance: One must unravel a thread upon entrance and follow its path to exit. So bravely taking up that thread and staying level-headed allows one to make it to freedom.

Errand into the Maze became a permanent part of the Graham repertory, and it also helped Martha overcome fear in her own life. Many years after she created that dance, the Graham company was on a plane in Iran bound for Teheran, Iran. They got caught in a snowstorm, and it seemed certain that the plane was going to crash. Martha forced her panic-stricken mind to recall another moment in which she had experienced fear but had gotten through it—performing *Errand into the Maze*. Over and over, she repeated the steps of the dance in her mind until the pilot miraculously managed to land the plane safely. And in 1988, when Martha had a stroke and overheard a doctor

Martha in Errand into the Maze, *a dance about overcoming one's fear and facing one's own destiny*

say, "At 94, people just don't come back,"[7] she kept herself alert by endlessly repeating the steps of *Errand into the Maze*.

In her autobiography, which she began when she was 90 years old, Martha thoughtfully chose that same dance as the first she would teach to children, because "it demonstrates . . . the strange place you are venturing into, something children might understand."[8] Martha loved children and realized that one of the main obstacles to a child becoming a confident adult is fear. She always encouraged children's curiosity.

The artist who designed the lighting for *Errand into the Maze* was Jean Rosenthal, who had studied at the Neighborhood Playhouse. Jean was as brilliant in her field as Martha was in hers. During the women's 37-year collaboration, Jean designed the lighting for 53 of Martha's productions. Jean's innovative lighting techniques were in constant demand, but she cherished working with Martha the most. "To do one or two new works for Martha a year was part of my life and a renewal of my own interior spirit,"[9] Jean said.

In the late sixties, when Jean was diagnosed with cancer and was suffering badly, she refused to stop working on the lighting for Martha's new dance. It was one of the few things that gave her strength. She was taken by ambulance to the theater to finish the lighting designs.

Jean, the sculptor Isamu, and Louis were touchstones for Martha. She never worried that they wouldn't understand what she wanted. These artists were on a level where they intuitively read Martha's thoughts. To have people such as these as collaborators and friends frees an artist to concentrate solely on creativity.

By 1948, Louis had been working with Martha for 22 years. But he was playing a less important role in the company as Erick took over more responsibilities. Louis had also been Martha's confidant, but this role, too, had been taken over by Erick. Finally, the collaboration ended. Martha and Louis remained good friends, and she still sought his advice. But the time just after they severed their working relationship was very painful for both of them. And even the dancers who had been criticized by Louis because of their drooped legs or mistakes during rehearsals missed his sharp eyes and comments.

Later that year, on September 20, 1948, Erick and Martha married. Then they drove to a Native American village in the Southwest. To start their marriage in a place that had given Martha so much inspiration seemed to bless the union.

Most of Martha and Erick's performances together were brilliant. In *Appalachian Spring*, the story of the frontier marriage, they didn't have to pretend they were deeply in love. But the pressures of their professional lives often intruded into their personal relationship. They spent almost every hour of every day together. When they were not practicing, they were doing administrative work. When they were not touring, they were rehearsing.

Being business associates and marriage partners is difficult for anyone, especially two sensitive artists with strong ambitions. Erick wanted to make his own name in the dancing world, but as long as he remained in Martha's dance company, he would always be known as one of the Graham dancers. Tensions arose between the two, despite the company's continued success. Then in 1950 they both were given the chance of a lifetime when Martha's friend Bethsabée offered to sponsor the company on a tour to London and Paris. The trip would cost more than $80,000, a fortune at that time.

The ballet world was centered in London and Paris. It had been in Paris that the riot had broken out over *The Rite of Spring* in 1913. Very little modern dance had been performed during the ensuing years.

In readying her company for this performance, Martha didn't redesign just one set of costumes— she overhauled the entire company wardrobe. For the next few months, the company was either stitching or rehearsing the four dances Martha chose to perform: *Errand into the Maze, Eye of Anguish, Cave of the Heart,* and *Every Soul Is a Circus.* Not a detail was overlooked in preparing for the departure to Paris. After all, the Graham company was also representing America. What was at stake, then, was no less than the name of America in the artistic world.

Just before leaving for Paris, Martha hurt her knee—a bad omen. In Paris, to the company's unpleasant surprise, they saw they had to perform on a stage that had an upward incline to it. These raked stages, as they are called, are common in Europe but not in America. The dancers had to adjust each dance to the unfamiliar stage in record time.

To add to the existing tension, former First Lady Eleanor Roosevelt and the most influential people in the dance and theater worlds from France, Italy, Spain, Scandinavia, and Eastern Europe all had tickets for opening night. Long before the curtain was to rise, the theater was overflowing with people.

There was no improvement in Martha's knee. *Cave of the Heart* is an extremely physically demanding dance. Several people pleaded with Martha to replace this dance or alter its difficulty, but Martha refused. The time came for the curtain to rise. Long after that time passed, the audience grew restless. What was going on? The former First Lady, Eleanor Roosevelt, had not arrived yet.

Eventually the show opened with *Errand into the Maze*. The audience did not react. *Eye of Anguish* received an even worse reception. Then came *Cave of the Heart*. Although pain was shooting through her body with every single movement of the knee, Martha was so much in control that not a soul in the audience knew it. At the end came *Every Soul Is a Circus*. During a jump, Martha came down sharply on the bad knee, and her leg collapsed.

By the time the dance was over, Martha's knee was the size of a grapefruit. She probably felt like crawling into bed and crying herself to sleep. But she could not disappoint all the fans eagerly awaiting her at the party in honor of her company.

The next day, the company had to rearrange the program without its star. Reviews were bad, and the morale of the company was even worse. Martha's knee showed no improvement. In this state, the most famous American modern dance company traveled on to London. Some people advised Martha to end the tour. Others advised her to continue, but not to dance herself. Still others said that if she didn't perform, the performances would be a failure. What did Martha think? She gritted her teeth, ignored the pain, and started rehearsals. During dress rehearsal, she reinjured her knee. She did not dance in London on opening night.

The trip was a failure. And it was also during this trip that her marriage to Erick collapsed. All of Martha's dreams were unraveling, and for the first time in her life, Martha was unable to do anything about it.

Chapter / Eight

Overcoming Obstacles

For the first time in her career, Martha was unable to dance. Although she refused to accept this fact, the pain that shot through her body with the slightest weight on the knee forced her to admit the truth. Specialist after specialist wanted to operate. At that time, this type of surgery was uncommon, and there was no guarantee that Martha would walk without a limp, let alone be able to dance again. Although inwardly she feared she might never dance again, she remained steadfast in her refusal to have surgery: "I won't have a violation done to my body."[1]

Downhearted, Martha took refuge in the Southwest. Perhaps the desert, with its silence and wide-open land, would have a healing, soothing effect on her soul and on her knee. In Santa Fe,

New Mexico, Martha sought the opinion of another doctor. She prepared herself to be told once again that she needed an operation. This doctor, however, realized that such a brilliant choreographer and dancer had to know a thing or two about the body. Instead of operating, the doctor and Martha worked out a system of rehabilitative treatments.

Part of Martha's therapy involved lifting weights with a sling attached to her leg. Each day at the same time, Martha lifted very light weights. She performed the exercises with the same discipline she utilized in creating her art. Martha kept up her regimen when she returned to New York. Her two dachshunds, Allah and Madel, would lay their warm bodies across her injured knee. She said that their loving care also played a major role in helping her to heal.

"I got to the point where I could put a typewriter on a sling and lift it with my leg. When I was able to lift 25 pounds, I was healed,"[2] said Martha. It was a remarkable recovery, one that would have been impossible for someone without as strong a will and discipline as Martha's. She later utilized the knowledge she gained to help other dancers with injuries. They sought her advice on how to heal themselves. The doctor in

New Mexico had been right; she did know a thing or two about the body and the way it functions.

In January 1951, almost a year after the accident, Martha was back on the stage—at one of the most prestigious American stages, Carnegie Hall—performing in *Judith*. Martha's knee, however, was not totally healed. Still she chose to perform the truest test of a dancer's skills, the solo. In a solo, all eyes are upon the artist, who can't afford to make a single mistake. Obviously, tremendous physical strength is required.

Most solos last about 5 minutes; 15 minutes is highly unusual. Martha's was 20 minutes long! Could she withstand such a test? A standing ovation at the end of the solo was answer enough. At 56 years old, Martha had made a miraculous comeback!

The *Judith* solo that so riveted people was an epic portrayal of war, love, and betrayal. In the ancient Biblical story, Judith saves the nation of Israel from its enemy, Holofernes. Judith was a very wealthy, beautiful woman whose husband had recently died. As was the custom, she wore rags and mourned her beloved husband. But Israel was in the middle of a terrible battle, which it was losing. The head of the Israelites begged Judith to do what they could not—conquer the enemy.

Their plan? Judith must turn her charms on Holofernes so that he would fall in love with her. Once they were alone in his tent, at the right moment, she had to kill him by driving a nail through his head. Judith executed the mission, and thus Israel was saved.

To perform that solo and find the best way to portray Judith, Martha read everything she could find about the ancient heroine. She discussed the character with psychologists and biblical experts. She got to know the character so well that she could imagine how Judith would act in any given situation. In short, she became Judith.

Nothing could take her out of character during performances. Years after she had originated the role, she said how difficult it had been to perform at Constitution Hall in Washington, D.C. Brass rings for electrical outlets jutted up onto the performance floor. Martha said she had feared catching her toe and falling. Walter Terry, the dance critic, said, "I thought you said you never thought of anything onstage, that you became the character itself." Martha replied, "It's true. I looked at those rings and said to myself, 'One more hazard for Judith to face.'"[3]

Despite being able to overcome her knee injury, Martha could not overcome the lack of funds needed for a permanent home for her company and school. That changed in 1952, when Martha's friend Bethsabée de Rothschild gave her a permanent home for the Martha Graham Dance Company and School of Contemporary Dance—a three-story building located at 316 East 63rd Street.

Rarely had such a costly contribution been given to an artist. But Bethsabée understood how Martha was inspiring hundreds of thousands of people with her dance and school. It would be unthinkable not to provide her with stability and room for growth.

The Graham company eagerly moved into the three-story brick building, which was overgrown with deep-green ivy. Little gardens fronted both sides of the building. On the second floor were offices, dressing rooms, and showers for the dancers. The most important activity took place on the first floor in the two dance studios. Both were airy and sunny, with back doors that opened up into the garden. To the side of the larger studio was Martha's tiny office. When she looked outside, she noticed a sapling growing in the path of her fence's wire gate. People wanted to uproot the tree, but Martha loved it so much that she allowed it to grow.

Martha's sister Geordie oversaw student

Martha rehearsing with her dancers in the studio

enrollment. Now that the Graham company had a stable home, it could maintain a scholarship program to ensure Martha her choice of talented dancers for her company.

Martha had just one obstacle to overcome: returning to Europe. She feared returning to the cities that had left such searing wounds on her psyche. And the loss of Erick still pained her deeply. Yet if she didn't tackle Europe, she would be giving into fear, which would mean she had no faith in her work. So, in March 1954, Martha took the plunge and toured the European cities of London, Copenhagen, Berlin, Paris, and Florence.

This time, there was no knee injury to hinder her performance. Publicity about Martha's return to Paris was at a fever pitch. The theater was again filled. And Martha didn't disappoint her audience. They loved her! At each stop on the tour, Martha and her company were heralded as gifted artists. Her confidence grew, especially when the American ambassador to Belgium telephoned and said that if Martha didn't perform there, it would cause problems in the relations between America and Belgium. He explained that the Belgians would ask why their country did not rate a stop on the tour. Martha solved what could have become a diplomatic issue by agreeing to perform in Belgium.

The news media flooded Martha with requests for interviews. People wanted to know how the mind of a person who had established such a revolutionary way of dancing worked. During her interviews, Martha credited one person not on the tour for playing an instrumental role in stimulating her creativity. This man, the friend from the beginning of Martha's career, was Louis Horst. In a letter to him, she revealed how happy all the positive attention made her. One person had even driven on a motorbike all the way from the Arctic Circle to see her perform, she noted. In England, a man named Robin Howard so loved Martha's work that he came to every London performance. He invited

Martha as well as her company to an Elizabethan feast. Martha sat at the queen's throne. She probably looked more the queen than the queen herself did and still had plenty of fun, too.

About seeing Martha in concert, Howard said, "I was completely bowled over. It was one of the greatest—perhaps *the* greatest—theatrical evenings in my life . . . and I vowed I would never look at dance again until I brought the Graham company back to London."[4] He did so in 1963, at considerable personal expense.

In Florence the Graham company had to share a program with an opera company. Opera is one of the most adored forms of entertainment for Italians, and the audience let Martha's company know. Their disapproval during the performance was so evident to Martha that for perhaps the first time in her life she went out of character and responded. "I raised my hand and the audience stopped. In my hand was the ability to halt their behavior; one movement."[5]

When the audience misbehaved again, Martha repeated the gesture. Again the audience grew silent. When the performance ended, Martha turned to her dancers and instructed, "No one bows this evening. No one. Keep your eyes on the floor and stand perfectly still."[6] The dancers obeyed. The audience was surprised, especially when the curtain came down. There was a moment of silence, then the audience burst into applause. The curtain rose, then fell, and then went up again, and still the company did not bow.

Finally, Martha walked to the front of the stage. She turned her back on the audience and bowed to her company. "I had no more trouble from then on,"[7] she said. In fact, the company returned six times to Florence to high critical acclaim and sold-out houses.

After Martha's first success overseas, she toured Europe regularly. Pan American Airlines even supplied the company with a plane at no charge to transport the dancers, costumes, and sets. The impact Martha had on the European dance world cannot be underestimated. The Europeans began to accept modern dance as an art equally as important as classical ballet. The first modern dance schools established in Europe were based on the Graham Technique. European dancers came to America with one goal in mind: to study with Martha. When they returned to their own countries, they set up companies or taught based on Graham Technique style.

Chapter / Nine

Giving the Gift of Dance

During Martha's groundbreaking European tour, she visited theaters and museums funded by various European governments. These governments believed that art was essential to the health of their society. The governments included in their budgets support for all the arts, from ballet schools for young children to opera houses, orchestra halls, and theaters. These provisions were never eliminated, even if a country went into a depression.

In America, there was no such budgeting. The arts were considered a luxury in the United States, which caused many artists to find themselves in positions similar to Martha's—highly renowned for their art and almost as highly in debt. An anonymous poet whom Martha quoted probably summed up her view about the attitude of the United States. That person wrote of a people who had disappeared from the face of the earth: "They had no poet and so they died / For the record of history lives through the arts."

The Soviet government had begun sending its state-supported, world-famous Kirov and Bolshoi ballet companies on world tours. Through these impressive cultural presentations, the Soviet leaders hoped to convince other nations that their government was not one of the most repressive in the world. These tours didn't sit well with the United States, the Soviet Union's rival. The two countries were in the midst of the Cold War, and both competed to be the world's number-one superpower. The United States government responded to its rival's tours by creating State Department tours. The more altruistic members of Congress explained that for there to be peace in the world, all nations must understand and accept one another's cultures. What better way to promote this idea than through the arts?

And so it was that in 1955, Martha prepared for her first U.S. State Department tour. It would take her to Japan, the Philippines, Thailand, Indonesia, Burma, India, Iran, and Israel.

Martha was no longer afraid to perform abroad, but other people feared for her. Many of the countries Martha would visit were hostile to the United States and unfamiliar with modern dance. What would happen if they didn't like Martha's dances?

Martha, however, could not wait to visit these nations and see their own native dances. She knew that these people had their own forms of dance, developed centuries before America had even become a nation. In fact, in the Hindu religion of India, it was Shiva, Lord of the Dance, who had created the universe.

Martha knew the company would have to travel with an interpreter, but as for the dance, she said, "I am not interested whether they understand or not. I am only interested if they feel it."[1] She knew that the language of art, in particular that of dance, is universal. Warmly clasp the hand of a Japanese or Indian without speaking, and the person will know you are opening yourself in welcome. Leap as though you just got the most wonderful news in your life, and those same people will understand that you are happy. Dance, Martha said, was the hidden language of the soul.

Of course, Martha was right. When she performed throughout Asia, an outcry arose that echoed all the way back to the White House. Why had America concealed such a national treasure as the Martha Graham Dance Company for so many years? The State Department did its best to rectify the situation by making sure that the 1955 tour was the first of many.

American diplomats acknowledged Martha as a cultural ambassador. When she received the Dance Magazine Award in 1957, she was called the "greatest single ambassador we have ever sent to Asia."[2] Politicians said she had done more for positive international relations than all the diplomats and American dollars had.

In every foreign country, the company performed to sold-out houses. At one tour stop, the people stampeded just to see Martha—when she wasn't even performing! In another country, Buddhist monks staged a sit-down strike until they were allowed entrance to a sold-out performance. Extra shows were added in other countries to accommodate Martha's many fans. In Thailand the company gave a special performance on the lawn of one of the prince's estates. In Iran the shah requested that they perform at his palace.

In Indonesia, one newspaper that had been

anti-American before Martha's company appeared wrote, "We always thought of America as the land of the bomb, the gadget, and the dollar. Martha Graham has shown us that America has a soul."[3] After the performance in Japan, the normally restrained citizens set off fireworks and threw confetti on the stage, and when the company left, the audience wept.

Martha's only complaint? Not enough time to meet with all the government dignitaries, visit all the students, and speak with all the fellow dancers who wanted to see her. Experiencing so many different cultures was a great gift for Martha. She witnessed each country's best dancers perform for her. She was escorted to historical sites, to museums, and to the best restaurants, where she and her dancers experienced a variety of foreign foods. Although some of her dancers got stomachaches, Martha was immune. And somehow, she managed to find time to shop the markets for presents for friends back in the States.

Perhaps another reason that people understood Martha's dance wherever she went was because of what Martha called blood memory. She defined this as the memories that our ancestors pass down throughout the centuries to our parents and, consequently, to us. The line extends back to the beginning of humankind. Even some of our insights or instinctive gestures come from some long-distant past, she explained. Blood memories are not conscious but come from the unconscious. The unconscious is the part of us responsible for our dreams. Our deepest desires and fears, our fantasies and darkest secrets are stored there as well.

Martha knew that much of our behavior is also motivated by the unconscious. Under the surface of good manners, Martha knew, was that hidden, sometimes barbaric part of each of us. Since she was interested in bringing to light the darkness, Martha chose heroines whose behavior was motivated by the unconscious as demonstrated in her cycle of dances based on Greek mythology.

The dynamic portrayals sometimes had unexpected results. The dance *Phaedra*, which premiered in 1962, so provoked two members of Congress, Senator Edna Kelley of New York and Congressman Peter J. Freylinghuysen of New Jersey that they protested in Washington. The dance revealed too much body and should not be allowed to tour with the State Department sponsorship, they complained.

The story that Martha had turned into a dance was about Phaedra, who falls in love with her stepson. She feels guilty over it, but as her

Martha performing in Clytemnestra, *one of her cycle of dances based on powerful women in Greek mythology*

passion is stronger, she confesses her love to him. When he rejects her, her love turns to hate, and she takes revenge by accusing him of seducing her. Her husband believes her and is so enraged that he kills his own son. Phaedra realizes that she is to blame for the murder and feels so guilty about it that she kills herself.

Even before *Phaedra* was attacked, Martha made her views on censorship very clear. "There are always people on the side of death, people whose energies are a little depleted, who desire the status quo. Exploration in the arts, as in other phases of life, is too painful for them. Their attitude is the symbol of a tired mind. . . . They attack anything new and disturbing. . . . These people think they can tear down the creative exploration of modern dancers. . . . They may make things infinitely more difficult for individuals. They may delay progress. But they will deepen the content of contemporary dances in the process and they will ultimately fail,"[4] she wrote in *Dance Magazine* in 1953.

Martha called a press conference to reiterate her beliefs. She also made a point that explained the use of the beauty of the body in *Phaedra*. "I have always thought 'eroticism' was a beautiful word. . . . Only hidden things are obscene. . . . I do things the way I see them. If others don't like it, they don't have to watch."[5]

A filmmaker named Nathan Kroll wanted even more people to watch Martha's works. In 1956, he asked to film her company. To his surprise, Martha refused. She was used to performing for a live audience, not for a mechanical camera eye. It took two years to convince her. And then, when the time came for Martha to appear on-camera, she got stage fright, locked herself in her dressing room, and wouldn't come out.

It looked like the project would have to be scrapped. And then the directors came up with a brilliant solution. Give Martha something to do while she's talking: Have her dressing for a performance. Martha found the solution satisfactory. The film, *A Dancer's World*, opened with Martha talking and preparing herself to appear in *Night Journey*, one of her dances. As she powdered her nose, pinned the queen's hair up with gold pins, fastened the gold collar and bracelet, and put on her robes, she discussed dance. Next came her dancers performing, and at the film's end, the film again focused on Martha in the dressing room. When she finished, she stood up, and walked toward the door leading to the stage, and the film ended. *A Dancer's World* won international awards, and many more films would follow, but not right away.

Martha still didn't feel comfortable appearing on television. TV stations didn't like the fact that this great star refused to appear on-camera. They threatened to boycott her New York seasons if she wouldn't show her face. Her worried press agent, Thomas Kerrigan, would somehow manage to convince the news media to come to the studio. Camera operators and reporters would arrive and arrange their lights, their tape recorders, and the cameras to focus on Martha. But she would train their attention toward what her dancers were doing, and without even realizing it, the TV crews were filming exactly according to Martha's directions. Only in the very end did they realize that instead of getting a story about Martha, they had a film of her dancers with her voice-over.

Kerrigan marveled that someone could star on TV, a strictly visual medium, without appearing before the cameras even once. He called the selling of Martha's voice to television one of the greatest successes of his career.

So it seemed that Martha's magic worked with filmmakers as well as dancers. She got them to do whatever she wanted. How did she inspire the thousands of people who studied with her to do what they had never done before, to grow as they never had thought possible? What was her method?

First, through her example, students felt the same sense of importance and awe for dance that she did. Martha said her dancers were public servants with a great responsibility: to fulfill other people's dreams of who they could be. She said the dancers had to perform this "service" for people because sometimes they were unable to do it for themselves. She considered this service to be a great privilege and honor.

Martha also gave her dancers discipline. "Freedom comes with discipline, and there is only one freedom on the stage, or in a performing art, and that is the result of extreme discipline. . . . When Nijinsky [a famous ballet dancer] came through the window in *Spectre of the Rose*, he electrified Paris. How many leaps do you suppose were behind that one leap that made legend? Probably hundreds, day after day, year after year, to arrive at that absolute eloquence when the body rested in space, and when it looked like the first leap that was ever made in the world,"[6] said Martha.

Martha felt that until dancers can master the basics of the technique or movement, they are not free but are imprisoned by having to pay attention to how to do these movements. Only when the moves come as naturally as a yawn can a dancer begin to think about freedom. If a person misses her two-hour practice one day, practicing for four hours the next day wouldn't make up for it. The day has been lost.

Thanks to discipline, Martha's dancers experienced the joy of moving their bodies in ways that they had never thought possible. They also reaped the benefits of this hard work when they took their bows onstage to standing ovations. And appearing before an approving audience was exhilarating. "I get a great deal from an audience. . . . The power you receive from them is marvelous," said Martha.[7]

Her passion was contagious. To the children she loved to teach, she said, "Do what you are doing and be excited about what you are doing. Be the best in your world by what you do and love it."[8] If a dancer didn't feel like he or she absolutely had to dance, then that person wasn't meant to be a dancer, Martha would say.

Martha demonstrated what she meant by passion during rehearsals for *Embattled Garden*, which drew inspiration from the biblical story of the Garden of Eden. In *Embattled Garden*, Martha felt that the wild, primitive passion the dance called for was lacking. She took the place of the dancer who played Eve. When the dancer playing the snake jumped down from the tree, Martha didn't wait for him to grab her; she lunged at him, threw him backward across the floor, and didn't let up until the sequence was over. Without one word, Martha demonstrated beyond a shadow of a doubt the level the performers must reach to become even finer dancers. And the dancers became two of the Graham Company's finest dancers. Their names were Yuriko and Glen Tetley.

Yuriko was an American of Japanese ancestry. During World War II, she and thousands of other loyal American citizens were wrongfully interned because of their Japanese descent. Upon Yuriko's release, she traveled to New York, where she sewed costumes for Martha and started taking her classes. In 1944, she was accepted into the company and eventually became a principal dancer.

Glen Tetley first met Martha in 1947. He didn't work with her but became a lead dancer for the Joffrey Ballet. In 1958, after a long, exhausting tour, he returned to New York depressed, suffering from a knee injury, and not sure whether he should continue dancing. Then he took a class from Martha. She helped him overcome his depression, heal his knee, and restore his faith in dance. He happily joined the Martha Graham Dance Company.

Martha inspired through imagery and stories. One of her favorite tales was that of the little sapling outside her studio window. Instead of dying when it confronted the wire gate of the fence, the tree had grown upward with the wire gate embedded in it. Martha said that this was the story of the dancer. Against all odds, the tree overcame its obstacle, reaching toward the heavens, just like those dancers who overcame the odds to become virtuoso performers. She meant that the dancer must be as strong and determined as that tree, no matter what obstacle he or she encounters.

Imagery as emotion plays an important part in Martha's landmark dance *Deaths and Entrances*. A woman in a black evening gown does a series of backward falls when the lover who rejected her enters the room. When someone said that this was unrealistic and that she would never do such a thing, especially in an evening gown, Martha replied that she wouldn't either, "but haven't you ever been in a room where someone you loved, who no longer loved you, walked in, and your heart fell to the floor?"[9] That's what she meant when she said her dancers revealed the hidden language of the soul.

She told her students, "Dancers never fall to fall, they fall to rise." After seeing Martha's company perform, Dame Margot Fonteyn, one of the world's finest classical ballet dancers, said, "Why, we [ballet dancers] fall like paper bags. You fall like silk."[10]

For a ballet knee bend, the demi-plié, in which the neck must be held up, Martha said, "Think that there are diamonds on your collar-bone for catching the light."[11] About the body, she said, "Just look at the way the ears rest next to the head; look at the way the hairline grows; think of all the little bones in your wrist. It is a miracle. And the dance is a celebration of that miracle."[12]

She likened the relationship of a dancer to her body to that of a musician to his instrument. "Learn it . . . as a musician learns his and becomes aware of all its little selfness. He uses it. He loves it. He handles it. He cherishes it. He watches it. He listens to it. A dancer does the same thing, he listens to his body."[13]

When Martha said something, she also got bodies to obey—even when her demands defied the laws of human nature. During one class, a nonprofessional student started to sweat and the dye from his shorts began forming a blue puddle on the newly resurfaced floor. Martha didn't look at him, for she would never embarrass someone for something he couldn't help. However, she stopped the class and said, "I forbid you to perspire. It's only self-indulgence." The student stopped sweating because, he said, "I was too scared of her to disobey her."[14]

Yet as long as a person was honest, there was nothing to fear from Martha. "She'd never test you in conversations. You felt totally comfortable about asking her anything, which is rare in people. . . . She made me feel the comfort of just being me,"[15] said Mikhail Baryshnikov, a Kirov Ballet principal dancer who defected from the Soviet Union and who later performed as a guest with Martha's company.

Martha emphasized that mind and body must be in harmony. She talked about the inner side of human beings and the outer side, the body. She said that just as what happens inside a house is more important than what happens or how it looks outside, the same is true for the human being. Regarding teaching, Martha wrote in her autobiography, "I would like to feel that I had, in some way, given them [dancers] the gift of themselves."[16]

Chapter / Ten

An Acrobat of God Faces Her Biggest Test

By 1959, Martha's career had spanned 43 years. If she had never created another dance, never taught another class, or never added another movement to her technique, she would still have been considered one of the greatest artists of the twentieth century.

Yet surprising the dance world was certainly not off-limits to Martha. That's exactly what she did when she agreed to collaborate with the world-famous classical ballet choreographer George Balanchine. Martha and George, at opposite ends of the dance spectrum, were supposed to create a dance called *Episodes*.

Of the odd pairing, Martha said, "My quarrel has never been with the ballet . . . perhaps to your amazement. I haven't been interested in destroying anything. I'm too busy doing something else."[1] Martha knew that classical ballet was the more popular of the two arts and that Balanchine's New York City Ballet was one of the best in the country. Working with that company could only gain modern dance an even wider audience.

George and Martha didn't collaborate in the usual manner, however; they did share the same program, the same music, and company dancers. But as for the choreography itself, each worked alone. Martha's dance would be performed in the first part, while George's would end the concert.

For her part, Martha chose to portray the historic power struggle between Mary, Queen of Scots, and her cousin, Elizabeth, the queen of England. The dramatic climax between the two queens comes in a high-stakes tennis match— death to the loser, the kingdom to the winner. Mary loses, but she accepts her fate with calmness, strength, and dignity. In so doing, Mary triumphs over her cousin in human spirit. Martha had the role of Mary, while Sallie Wilson of the New York City Ballet was Elizabeth.

Upon meeting Sallie, Martha said, "I'm terrified of you."[2] It wasn't because of Sallie's role as her executioner. It was because Sallie had no training in contemporary dance. The ballerina, however, had been taught to give the choreographer the exact style that she or he wanted, and she was talented enough to do so. What had seemed like a major obstacle was easily overcome.

Martha celebrated her sixty-fifth birthday in the studio rehearsing. A few days later on May 14, 1959, the curtain at the New York City Center rose for the premiere of *Episodes*. Before part one even began, the audience gave Martha a standing ovation. When the dance ended, the company had been directed not to take bows. The audience, however, would not stop clapping until Martha and her fellow performers took their bows.

With *Episodes*, Martha gained the wider recognition she had been hoping for. And she was just as much a heroine as the characters she played, for she had performed the role in great pain. She had arthritis, an inflammation of the joints, which causes pain in the affected areas. Martha had it in her hands and her feet, but she mentioned it to no one.

Dancing is the most physically demanding of all the arts. Martha was well over the age when most dancers are forced to retire. The thought of retiring terrified her so much that she refused to even consider the possibility. Yet it was becoming more difficult to perform at the level she once had.

Martha thought of dancers as athletes of God. As such, they should never have to retire. She testified to that fact in Acrobats of God, which premiered on April 27, 1960. Here the performers were truly acrobats, doing impossible things with their bodies. While the female dancers did deep knee bends on a slanted ballet barre, their partners did the same—upside down, standing on their hands. Martha played the role of choreographer, but each time a dancer turned to her for help, she hid behind a screen.

Martha had not intended for Acrobats to be a comedy, but it turned into one when she noticed during the premiere that the audience was laughing. She hammed it up and the other dancers took their cue from her. The result was another masterpiece. And thoughts of retirement were far from Martha's mind when, that same year, she received America's most prestigious honor for contribution to the field of dance, the Capezio Dance Award.

In 1963, Martha's schedule was so full that she and the company were out of the country touring more than they were in it. There was another U.S. State Department tour of the Middle East, Turkey,

In Acrobats of God, *Martha (lower right) portrayed a choreographer who hides when her dancers turn to her for help.*

Greece, Rumania, Yugoslavia, Poland, Finland, Sweden, Norway, Germany, and the Netherlands. Martha was also commuting to Israel to help Bethsabée establish the Batsheva Dance Company. In September of that year, Martha's company returned to England, where critics called her program one of the most amazing experiences for any theatergoer.

Among the well-wishers backstage in London was the world's finest classical ballet dancer, Rudolf Nureyev. He had defected from the Soviet Union during a government-sponsored tour with the Kirov Ballet and was now a principal dancer for England's Royal Ballet. Instead of praising Martha, however, Rudolf said nothing. For once, her powers of detecting what a person was thinking failed. While Martha wondered if he didn't like the dance or couldn't speak English, she was too polite to ask.

December 1963 found Martha in Detroit where, along with Louis Horst, she received an honorary doctorate in the humanities from Wayne State University, the first of many she received. As Louis had never graduated from high school, this recognition of his talents meant a lot to him. About one month later, Martha showed how much she cared by throwing him a huge party for his eightieth birthday. Martha herself was almost 70.

Less than one week later, Louis collapsed and was rushed to the hospital. His health did not improve, and on January 23, 1964, Martha's close friend died. Never again would Louis tease about "little pink toes," as he called the dancers he taught. Never again would Martha be able to call Louis for advice. She had lost one of her greatest friends, one who had composed the scores for several of her masterpieces, including *Frontier*, *Primitive Mysteries*, and *El Penitente*.

"His sympathy and understanding, but primarily his faith, gave me a landscape to move in.

Without it, I should certainly have been lost. . . . He was the great influence in American dance, and those who have been touched by his thoughts are richer for it. To many dancers he has been father, priest, confessor, and I'm proud and honored to have been among the first," Martha wrote in the January 29, 1964, edition of *The New York Times*.[3]

The magazine Louis had founded, *Dance Observer*, ceased publication upon his death. The last issue, January 1964, had on its cover Martha and Louis in caps and gowns receiving their honorary doctorates. While Louis's passing hurt Martha so much that she could hardly talk about him, she was able to honor him in a way that spoke most eloquently of her feelings for him— through her dance. The Connecticut College Summer School of Dance sponsored the Louis Horst Memorial Concerts in the summer of 1964.

In preparing for the memorial performances, Martha was confronted by several problems. The choreography for *Primitive Mysteries* and *Frontier*, for which Louis composed the musical scores, had never been written down. No one in the current company knew the dances since they hadn't been performed in years. Martha knew them, but she had to be in Israel to work with the Batsheva. She also found it too painful to work on these dances because they brought back so many memories of her departed friend—and because she herself could not perform the physical moves of the dances anymore.

Martha assigned to her rehearsal director, David Wood, what seemed to be the impossible task of recreating the dances. There was one poor-quality film of the solo *Frontier* for dancer Ethel Winter to go by. All that was left of *Primitive Mysteries*, however, was Louis's musical score. David despaired until he realized he had an invaluable resource to turn to—the memories of the dancers who had performed in those roles years before.

David called members of Martha's early concert group to help. They came from all over the United States, eager to do whatever they could. Each woman remembered her own part, and Sophie Maslow, who had studied Martha's every move as the Virgin, was able to reconstruct this role. Bit by bit, phrase by phrase, *Primitive Mysteries* was reborn.

In the end, everything came together smoothly for the Memorial Concerts, and in her speech Martha said that Louis would have liked the fact that people were celebrating him in this manner. As for her own self, watching others perform in the roles she had originated was like a part of her was being ripped away. Not only was Martha no longer physically capable of dancing these roles, she was in poor health. She tried to hide it, denying one of her earliest lessons from childhood—that the body never lies. People saw through her behavior.

Martha then began choreographing new works that were less demanding and more theatrical. Critics didn't approve. Attendance at her concerts dropped. Age was the one obstacle that all of Martha's effort and determination could not overcome. A few critics suggested that Martha retire.

Martha was very troubled during this time—and full of self-doubt. She said to someone that she wasn't a very good choreographer and didn't know how to teach, but she was a dancer and had to be a dancer. If dance was taken away from her, she would have nothing. But if Martha allowed things to continue as they were, soon there would be nothing left of the Martha Graham Dance Company.

Things came to a head in 1970 when the Brooklyn Academy of Music (BAM) again invited the company to appear but required that the repertory include some of Martha's earlier masterpieces. Only her younger dancers were capable of performing in those physically demanding roles, not Martha herself, so she resisted. But some of the dancers informed her that the company wanted to appear without her. And since the Martha Graham Dance Company was a nonprofit, tax-exempt corporation, the board of directors had the final say in matters such as these. Martha was overruled and settled into resigned acceptance.[4]

On opening night, October 2, 1970, Martha watched in the wings as her company performed at the Brooklyn Academy of Music. The same evening she was awarded New York City's highest honor for cultural achievement, the Handel Medallion. During her acceptance speech she vowed to be back onstage the following spring. She was 76 years old.

Instead, Martha fell very ill and had to be hospitalized. All the years of working herself so hard and all the strain she had put her body through finally caught up with her. She was diagnosed as having diverticulitis, an intestinal disorder. Her physical illness was compounded by her depression.

For the next year and a half, she fought for her life while her company and school fought for theirs. There were no more tours. With no promise of performing professionally, many well-known company stars left. Student enrollment fell off. No income was coming in. For the first time, the company had to hold open auditions to find dancers. Before, dancers had risen through the ranks of the Martha Graham School of Contemporary Dance. The Graham Technique was second nature to them by the time they joined the company. Not so for many of the new dancers.

A limited repertory because of Martha's refusal to restore older dances compounded company problems. To ensure the survival of the existing dances and keep the company from sinking into oblivion, Bertram Ross and Mary Hinkson, as associate artistic directors, staged studio workshop performances.

For a world-class company, this was a major step backward. Only companies just starting out did such things. Martha herself never did it; she had started out on Broadway. But the alternative for the company was far worse—to disband. It was thanks in large part to Mary and Bertram that the company survived during this difficult time.

Many doubted that Martha would ever recover, let alone come back to head her company. And then, "one morning, I felt something welling up within me. I knew that I would bloom again," said Martha.[5] Just as surely as she had fought her way out of the labyrinth in *Errand into the Maze*,

Martha fought her way back to health. When she had a hairdresser come to the hospital to dye her hair black, since it had gone white during her illness, her friends took this as a sure sign that she would be rejoining the ranks of the living.

Upon release from the hospital, she rigorously followed her doctor's orders. For the disciplined Martha, this was easy. Not so easy was the challenge of restoring the repertory, the company, and the school to their former prestige. Martha would also have to come up with a really great dance to prove to the critics that she was still capable of choreographing masterpieces.

She tackled that challenge as she had tackled so many before. She pulled her dark hair back in a bun, put on makeup, dressed elegantly, and slowly, with dignity, walked to the front of the studio to begin rehearsals with many company dancers whom she had never met. Instead of sitting on the floor, Martha sat in a chair, and for the first time she did not show the dancers what to do. Demonstrators did that for her now.

The dancers had almost as tough a challenge as Martha did. They knew they would be compared to former great company dancers and wanted to measure up favorably. They practiced day and night. Would all their effort be enough to get them into shape for a Broadway season? Would they be able to fill the house?

Martha decided they would. She created two new works and revived several earlier classic dances. Finally, in May 1973, the curtain at the Alvin Theater rose on the Graham dancers. The company had been away from Broadway for four long years. If the season was successful, Martha would resume her position as head of the most celebrated modern-dance company in America. If not, her career could be over.

Martha watched her dancers perform from the wings, and despite all the pressure, she was happy this time just to be there. When the curtain came down on opening night, the members of the audience rose and cheered. Martha had done it again! One critic wrote that she had been reborn and the world of modern dance along with her. Her dancers, critics said, were not simply imitating roles performed years earlier, they were renewing them and enhancing them with their own individuality.

Despite all the external praise, things within the company were not going so well. When Martha had returned to take charge, she had made Ron Protas executive director. Ron had supported her during her illness, but people associated with the company resented this newcomer. Martha herself seemed changed. To many friends and associates, she was unavailable and making decisions with which they did not agree. Bertram Ross and Mary Hinkson, the artistic directors during Martha's illness, left, as did some of the other veteran dancers. Some administrators and people on the board of directors also left. Hard feelings between Martha and her former associates would remain for years.

By 1974, the transformation of Martha Graham and her company and its administrators was complete. Tensions were gone. The school was growing steadily, and the company embarked on a tour of Europe and the Far East. The phoenix had arisen from the ashes—and she was 80 years old.

Chapter / Eleven

More Milestones

While functioning in the red was typical for almost every modern-dance company, the debts at the Graham company and school were out of control. Martha was against holding a benefit concert for the company and school, but the board of directors basically forced her hand. "I hated to admit that we couldn't make money in a more natural way,"[1] said Martha.

The benefit, on June 19, 1975, would also kick off the yearlong celebration of the company's fiftieth anniversary. Ticket prices ranged from $50 to $10,000. For that kind of money, Martha needed not only to premiere a new work but also to fill the bill with star performers. Martha found a typically unorthodox solution to the challenge. She asked ballet star Rudolf Nureyev to be a guest artist. He was the same classical dancer who hadn't said a word to Martha after the company's 1963 performance in England.

To Martha's delight, Nureyev agreed. His friend Dame Margot Fonteyn, the famous classical ballet dancer, also agreed to be a guest artist. And both refused any payment for performing the dance Martha choreographed especially for them, entitled *Lucifer*. They likely felt as did Mikhail Baryshnikov, who later performed as a guest artist, when he explained why he danced for no fee: "Listen, to dance with a company like that is a privilege . . . It's the chance of a lifetime."[2] During that time Rudolf also finally explained why he hadn't spoken to Martha after her performance in 1963: He'd been so moved that he was speechless.

The two biggest names in the ballet world were scared to death of working with Martha. And the biggest name in modern dance was just as frightened of them. There may have been some truth to her joke that they'd all get along fine if they didn't kill one another first. Yet as soon as Fonteyn's and Nureyev's feet touched the studio floor, the magical interaction between choreogra-

Mikhail Baryshnikov in knee pads—to protect his knees from
injury— leaps above Martha during rehearsal.

pher and dancers began, and there was no room left for fear.

Martha didn't give them any breaks just because they were stars, either. When Rudolf was 30 minutes late for rehearsal, Martha said she was angry. The other dancers, perhaps aware of her temper, quickly moved to the sides of the studio, leaving Rudolf alone to face Martha. She proceeded to demonstrate to Rudolf that artists, no matter how acclaimed, are not exempt from being civil to their fellow human beings. In plain terms, she said that by being late, the greatest ballet dancer in the world was behaving like a spoiled child. Rudolf apologized and was never late again.

Anticipation of the upcoming benefit was so great that weeks before the show, every single ticket was sold. Luckily, Martha had thoughtfully set aside many less costly tickets for her students. On the big night, the countless limousines pulling up to the Uris Theater snarled traffic for blocks. They delivered celebrities in the arts, sciences, and politics. Photographers and reporters jostled with one another to take pictures and get quotes from the gloriously attired theatergoers. Secret Service agents guarded the theater's front doors. Their presence was necessary because one of the attendees was First Lady Betty Ford.

Years before Mrs. Ford became the First Lady, she had studied with Martha at Bennington. She also appeared in 1938 at Carnegie Hall in *Appalachian Spring*. The First Lady spoke for many who knew Martha when she said, "She helped shape my life. She gave me the ability to stand up to all the things I've had to go through, with much more courage than I ever would have had without her."[3] Acclaimed actress Joanne Woodward, another attendee and former student of Martha's, credited her for helping inspire her own career.

Just before the show began, the curtain rose on Martha. She wore an elegant, long, emerald-green gown. The audience instantly hushed. She directed the technicians to turn up the lights on the audience so that she could see her friends. In a warm, low voice, Martha began to talk about dance: "A dancer is a flame in the world. . . . A dancer need not live a monastic life. Heaven forfend, I'm hungry for every sensation I can get." Of the unspoken questions about her age, she said, "Age is relative. I've noticed some girls [of 16] who are older than ladies of 60."[4]

While Martha admitted that she would rather be dancing, her theatricality and emotion found their outlets in these few precious moments onstage. Once again, the audience was riveted, for she was as charismatic as she had been as a dancer at the peak of her abilities. And the flame of which Martha spoke was evident in the dancers' performance.

The benefit ended to standing ovations. And at perhaps her tenth interview of the evening, Martha said, "I'm a little overwhelmed, because I've never had such an array of cameras and such glamour treatment in my life. Even if this is just Cinderella for a night."[5]

The event raised more than anyone had thought possible—$200,000—the largest amount raised in one night in the history of dance. And yet deficits remained in company coffers. The *Lucifer* ballet had cost $48,000 to mount. The cost of the costumes, studded with diamonds, gold, platinum, and other precious gems, was estimated at around $250,000.

Martha, however, did not have to pay for the costumes. The designer Halston designed them for free. Martha had met him when he agreed to lend her one of his glamorous dresses—something he never did—to wear when she presented the Capezio Dance Award to the musical director and principal conductor of the New York City Ballet, Robert Irving.

Martha loved the dress so much that she

didn't want to give it back. It was a soft, earth-colored cashmere, both comfortable and elegant. When Martha asked to pay for it in monthly installments, Halston refused, insisting she take the dress as a gift. Soon after, he began designing costumes for her dancers. Eventually, Halston redesigned the entire company wardrobe. Martha even wore his elegant, comfortable designs to rehearsals.

Martha and First Lady Betty Ford remained in touch after the benefit, for Mrs. Ford had agreed to be the honorary chairwoman of the fiftieth anniversary gala celebration, during the 1976 season. The four-week season at the Mark Hellinger Theater was the longest a dance company had ever had. The 1976 season also celebrated the sixtieth year of Martha's career, her one hundred fiftieth dance, and the fact that her 28-member company was the largest yet.

Martha dedicated the latest dance, *The Scarlet Letter*, to actress Katherine Cornell, who had funded Martha's first week-long Broadway season. In addition, Martha honored Aaron Copland by asking him to conduct the orchestra for *Appalachian Spring*—whose award-winning score he had composed. The performance coincided with his seventy-fifth birthday. When asked how he felt about it, Copland said, "Nervous." He hadn't conducted an orchestra since 1934!

After the Broadway season ended, the company embarked on a 20-week European tour. And good things kept happening. On October 15, 1976, Martha was again reunited with First Lady Betty Ford—at the White House. President Ford presented to Martha the Presidential Medal of Freedom, the highest civilian honor an American citizen can receive. Martha was the first dancer and choreographer to ever receive one.

At the White House, Martha and her fellow guests watched as the lead Graham dancer, Janet Eiber, performed *Frontier* and *Lamentation*. Afterward, Martha's presidential hosts held a black-tie dinner in her honor. One of the many friends in attendance was Frances Steloff, the bookstore owner who had loaned Martha $1,000 for her first concert. "You made a good investment,"[6] said President Ford to Frances, and he also hailed Martha as a national treasure.

The "national treasure" was showered with awards from all over the world. Throughout her life, Martha received close to 40 awards and honors. Among them were the New York Public Library Dance Collection's honors (1974), the Cathedral of St. John the Divine Award (1974), the Kennedy Center Honors Award (1979), the Samuel H. Scripps American Dance Festival Award (1981), the Knight of the French Legion of Honor (1984), the Carina Ari Medal from Sweden (1985), President Reagan's National Medal of Arts (1985), and the Order of the Precious Butterfly with Diamond from Japan (1990).

In 1984, Yuriko returned to the Graham company, not to dance but to help establish the Martha Graham Ensemble. The ensemble was an apprentice company that gave performances and demonstrations at schools and in the studio. Many members of the ensemble eventually became dancers in the company. All of them hoped to attain this goal and participate in the worldwide tours, including one in which Martha was privileged to have an audience with the Pope.

Despite the acclaim, Martha said, "I have never thought of myself as famous. I suppose I am, but you can't go around thinking of those things. I don't. I just go."[7] And go she did. She turned 90 in 1984! She was also very honest about her dances, and said, "There have been lots of clinkers,"[8] as well as the successful ones.

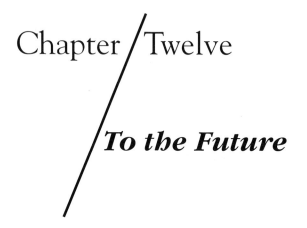

Chapter /Twelve

To the Future

"What on earth can one say about a national treasure who is still at the head of her own dance institution during its Diamond Jubilee [sixtieth anniversary] and is still choreographing?"[1] critic Clive Barnes wrote in 1986, noting that Martha's was the longest-running modern-dance company and school in the world.

Yet, at 92 years of age, Martha knew that she wouldn't be around forever. She now realized that her dances needed to be preserved for future dancers. With the help of her artistic directors, Ron Protas and Linda Hodes, the company had already begun to reconstruct and record on film some of her older works. The trouble was that many of the older dances were recorded only in her head. And by now she had created almost 200 works!

Martha wanted to create films that showed her technique, the dancers in rehearsal, and finally, in performance—a very expensive proposition. To do the job right, they needed major funding. The Graham School applied for a grant from the National Endowment for the Arts, but it didn't receive enough money to do the full project. Martha said it broke her heart. Then Arizona Senator Dennis DeConcini heard about the company's plight, and in 1987 he introduced a bill to appropriate $7 million to preserve Martha's works and renovate the school. The senator said, "She has received piddling little amounts [grants]. . . . It's just a shame not to preserve the woman's work on videotape for posterity."[2] Another congressman said that even if people disagreed about funding the project, they all agreed on Martha's greatness.

Congress decided against it, saying that it would create a precedent that would force government to fund other dance companies, which mostly operated at a deficit, too. Still the company used the funds it did receive to record as many dances as possible.

Then, in early January 1988, disaster struck. "One moment I was preparing to have a guest to tea, another unable to speak, but understanding everything,"[3] Martha wrote in her autobiography. She just managed to tell Ron Protas, who worked with her for 22 years, and her nurses that she was sorry.

Martha was rushed to the hospital. Just a few weeks before, she had been in Tucson, taking care of her ailing sister Geordie. Now she was the one stricken.

The doctors said that she had had a stroke, and at her age they were not sure how well she would come back. She actually overheard one young doctor saying her chances weren't very good. But the doctors didn't know how much of a fighter she was. She fought back with the help of the dance *Errand into the Maze*, keeping herself alert by constantly repeating the steps of the dance in her mind.

When Martha felt better, she informed the doctors that she was leaving the hospital. They told her she wasn't well enough yet. "I tried to explain that I had an entire company waiting for me to begin a new work in just seven days. It would be the best medicine,"[4] she wrote. In the end, Martha's opinion overruled that of the doctors, and she checked out of the hospital and into the rehearsal studio. Martha was sure that her new work, *Night Chant*, based on a Navajo healing ceremony, would help her recover. The dance premiered on October 13, 1988.

The season was successful but full of sadness for
Martha. First her sister Geordie died, and then in
December her good friend Isamu Noguchi also
passed away. Despite the grief that Martha felt, she
continued to work as often as she was able, including teaching the children's classes. The children,
aged 7 to 10, loved the expressive modern-dance
classes. When one youngster was asked what she
liked best about her classes, she answered, "I love it
all."[5]

An older, more famous fan, former First Lady
and book editor Jacqueline Kennedy Onassis,
asked Martha to write her autobiography, which

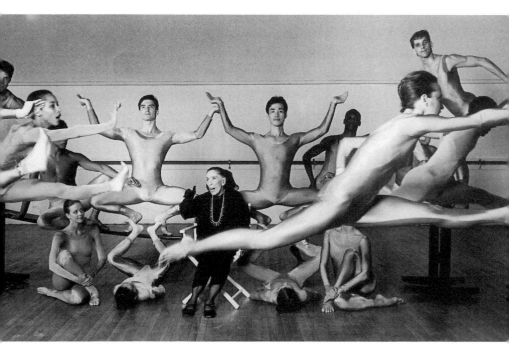

Martha, unable to dance, conducts a rehearsal while seated.

Martha had actually already been working on. She said others would find Martha's story inspiring enough to take on the challenge of fulfilling their own dreams. Martha's hands were so crippled by arthritis that she could not write. She recorded her story on tape instead. Others typed it for her.

It's true that at 96, Martha was frail. She often needed help to walk. But with her large, deep-set dark eyes, her elegant attire, her jaw's firm thrust, and her calm dignity, she seemed to emanate an aura of peace.

And she was still one of the world's most well-known choreographers. The Spanish government chose her to choreograph the dance for its 1992 celebration of Christopher Columbus's voyage to America 500 years before. Martha called the dance *The Eyes of the Goddess*. The central figure in the dance is death. The principal dancer, Kenneth Topping, said, "There was a section in which she wanted the dancers to deal with props that were to represent death to us. 'Feel about them however you feel about death,' she said. 'You may feel death is a sweet thing. I don't. I'm angry at it.'"[6]

Martha, who always so closely identified her life with her art, was having difficulty finishing *The Eyes of the Goddess*. She finally took a break from that particular dance, which resulted in the choreographing of her one hundred ninety-first dance, *Maple Leaf Rag*, to the tune of the same name by Scott Joplin. That music held wonderful memories for Martha, as many years earlier, Louis had helped her triumph over her choreographic blocks by playing the same lighthearted tune.

The dance premiered on October 2, 1990. *New York Times* dance critic Clive Barnes wrote that *Maple Leaf Rag* was witty, delicate, and light-hearted, and full of the spirit of an exuberant, extremely talented teenager. Not a bad review for Martha, who was nearing 100 years.

Among the well-wishers escorted backstage that season was the pop singer Madonna. Before Madonna became famous, she studied at the Graham school. In her autobiography, Martha wrote, "At first, [Madonna] would come two hours early to watch me come in."[7] Perhaps Madonna learned something from Martha about stage presence. Madonna admired the Martha Graham Dance Company so much that she had given it a gift of $150,000 two years earlier when Martha was recovering from her stroke. She also began discussing with producers the possibility of doing a movie about Martha, in which Madonna would play the lead.

Two weeks after the 1990 season ended, Martha and her company boarded a plane to Tokyo for a 55-day tour of the Far East. In Taipei, Taiwan, Martha held a party in honor of the company at the hotel. She left early, but instead of going to bed, she threw open the curtains of her hotel room and watched the party through her window. She enjoyed seeing others have a good time.

Then, while in Diamond Head, Hawaii, Martha fell ill again. She returned to New York in January 1991 and entered the hospital. There she remained through mid-March. At first she was thought to be recovering, but then her condition worsened. On April 1, Martha passed away in her home. *The Eyes of the Goddess* would not be finished by Martha. The goddess who had seemed immortal was gone.

The dance world mourned the passing of the greatest legend in modern dance. Her dancers grieved. They were like a family who had lost both parents.

Terese Capucilli, a lead company dancer, said, "Martha had been through so much, and we have seen her bounce back so often from illness, I always felt Martha was going to outlive us all. She will, I hope, in her work." Steve Rooks, another principal dancer, remembered that in the dance *Temptations of the* Moon, "I kept blowing it. . . .'Steve,' she said, 'get on your knees.' I thought she was going to show me something. And then she slapped me and said, 'You silly boy.' But it worked."

Joyce Herring, another lead dancer, remembered her last long conversation with Martha. It was in Seoul, South Korea, in Martha's hotel room. "She looked radiant, like a beautiful, innocent young girl," Joyce recalled. She was peeking out the

Martha surrounded by her dancers

window, excited with the hustle and bustle of the street below. "I love the light," Martha had said.[8]

As Martha had wished, there was no formal funeral service. Her ashes were scattered over the Sangre de Cristo Mountains in northern New Mexico, and on the anniversary of her birth, a mass was offered at a sanctuary in the Southwest, the place that had so inspired her during her life.

The unspoken question that the dancers and dance world had asked time and again before Martha passed on, now needed answering: What would the company do with Martha gone?

The answer was that it would go on, just as Martha had. On June 3, 1991, the Martha Graham Dance Company held a free memorial concert commemorating its founder. These were the words on the invitations to the concert: "You are invited to join other friends and supporters of the Martha Graham Dance Company at a special performance. . . . This performance was [Martha Graham's] wish of a gift to you."[9]

People came to remember Martha from across the United States. Former dancers, choreographers, longtime friends, and others who loved Martha filled the 2,500 seats of the auditorium on June 3. At 5:00 the curtain rose on 32 of the youngest students of the Martha Graham School of Contemporary Dance. The seven- to ten-year-olds wore white leotards. Exuberantly the children performed steps called triplets and saluted the sun, opening their bodies toward the sky. They demonstrated the moves' meanings by saying, "I love the sun. I love the earth. I love the world," lines Martha had borrowed from a Native American ceremonial dance. This section of the program was called "To the Future," which these young dancers represented.

Then, to an emotional audience and standing ovations, the members of the Martha Graham Dance Company performed *Maple Leaf Rag*, *Acts of Light*, *Errand into the Maze*, and *Primitive Mysteries*. When the program ended, the curtain remained up on the empty stage.

Although Martha was gone, the legacy she left enabled the Martha Graham Dance Company to endure—and to thrive. The company was already booked on tours of the United States, Europe, and the Far East for the next two years. Many influential people in the artistic fields came forward to support the company and ensure its survival. Some, like the premier classical ballet dancer Mikhail Baryshnikov, planned to dance as a guest artist in the company, despite his own busy schedule. Others, like philanthropist Doris Duke, generously donated money for the company. "I am honored to have been [Martha's] friend and to have experienced the power and spirit of her extraordinary creations," said Doris.[10]

In September 1991, Martha's autobiography, *Blood Memory*, was published. It coincided with the company preparing for the first season without her presence. When the season began, the dancers bowed slightly in unison toward the wings at stage right where Martha used to sit. On the program was the unfinished segment of Martha's last dance, *The Eyes of the Goddess*.

This first critical season without Martha was hailed as a success. Anna Kisselgoff, critic for the *New York Times*, wrote, "The truth is that the Graham company has a better chance of existing without its founder than other modern-dance groups and even most ballet companies. It can recruit from its own thriving school and has a wide repertory. . . . It performs in Graham's codified idiom—one that makes her work transferable from one generation of dancers to another."[11]

For new dances, highly regarded choreographers from different companies were invited to premiere a new work for the company each year. Twyla Tharp, a world-famous choreographer, premiered the contemporary ballet, *Demeter and*

The Eyes of the Goddess, *which Martha never lived to see on stage, was about death.*

Persephone, successfully during the 1993 season. Before she formed her own company, Tharp was a member of Merce Cunningham's Dance Company. Merce had gotten his start in Martha's company.

Eight members of the company demonstrated their own choreographic abilities on January 23, 1993, when they presented their works in a performance called the Choreographers Project. The 1993 season also celebrated the one hundredth anniversary of Martha's birth with new dances, new national and local projects, and renewed corporate support.

By the company's seventieth anniversary, in 1996, Ron Protas, the artistic director of the

company, says that he hopes 60 of Martha's contemporary ballets will have been restored for the
repertory.

Each year, in late summer, the Martha
Graham School of Contemporary Dance holds
auditions for full or partial scholarships. On audition day, the Graham School's narrow hallway is
lined with dozens of hopeful young dancers
waiting for a turn to give the performance of their
lives. They are as nervous as Martha was when she
auditioned for Miss Ruth St. Denis so many years
ago. They talk, giggle, stretch, and pray that they
will be one of the chosen. Some will be taken into
the Martha Graham Ensemble. The most talented
and dedicated may become members of the famed
Martha Graham Dance Company.

The school's summer session winds down soon
after auditions. The members of the Martha
Graham Dance Company haven't yet returned
from their vacations, and final decisions about
which dancers will play what parts in the upcoming season are being made. The building is very
quiet and peaceful. On these hot August days, the
window of Martha's former office is open. It faces
the garden, home of that once-tiny sapling whose
trunk grew around the wire gate.

With each passing year, the tree's green leaves

are reaching higher, filling more of the blue sky. The story of the tree that Martha used so many times to inspire dancers is the story of the Martha Graham Dance Company. Despite all obstacles, it grows bigger and stronger with each season, blossoming with life, and with it lives the legacy of Martha Graham.

Chapter Notes

Chapter 1

1. Martha Graham, *Blood Memory* (New York: Doubleday, 1991), 5.
2. Ibid., 18.
3. Ibid., 19.
4. Agnes de Mille, *Martha* (New York: Random House, 1991), 103.
5. Graham, *Blood Memory*, 19.
6. Ibid., 25.
7. Ibid., 34.
8. Ibid., 46.
9. Ibid., 41.
10. Don McDonagh, *Martha Graham: A Biography* (New York: Praeger, 1973), 15.
11. Mary Campbell, "Dancers Prefer to Keep Moving On," *News Tribune*, May 8, 1986, 28.
12. Graham, *Blood Memory*, 60.

Chapter 2

1. Graham, *Blood Memory*, 61.
2. Walter Terry, *Frontiers of Dance: The Life of Martha Graham* (New York: Thomas Y. Crowell Company, 1975), 27.
3. Martha Graham, Foreword to *Dance Drawings of Martha Graham*, by Charlotte Trowbridge (New York: *Dance Observer*, 1945).
4. Graham, *Blood Memory*, 67.
5. Ibid., 66.

6. Ibid., 69.
7. De Mille, 57.
8. Graham, *Blood Memory*, 79.
9. *Santa Barbara News*, October 2, 1920.
10. De Mille, 63.
11. Graham, *Blood Memory*, 86.
12. Campbell, "Dancers Prefer to Keep Moving On," *News Tribune*, May 8, 1986, 28.
13. Graham, *Blood Memory*, 93.

Chapter 3

1. "Martha Graham Reflects on Her Art and Life in Dance," *New York Times*, March 31, 1985, Sec. 2.
2. Joseph H. Mazo, "Martha Graham," Martha Graham 60th Anniversary Dance Journal, Martha Graham Dance Company, 1986.
3. Graham, *Blood Memory*, 108.
4. Ibid., 274.
5. Ibid., 113.
6. Ibid., 114.

Chapter 4

1. De Mille, 126.
2. Anna Kisselgoff, "Reflections on Martha Graham's Revolution," *New York Times*, May 29, 1988.
3. Graham, *Blood Memory*, 114.

4. De Mille, 90.
5. John Martin, Dance Critic, *New York Times*, March 1929.

Chapter 5

1. Dorothy Bird, speech given at Dance Critics Association Conference, June 1982.
2. De Mille, 130–131.
3. From the film *The Early Years: American Modern Dance from 1900 through the 1930s.*
4. Ibid.
5. Jennifer Dunning, "Martha in Present Tense," *New York Times*, September 25, 1994, Sec. 2.
6. Marian Horosko, *Martha Graham: The Evolution of Her Dance Theory and Training 1926–1991* (Chicago: Chicago Review Press, 1991), 78.
7. De Mille, 151.
8. Graham, *Blood Memory*, 120.
9. McDonagh, 53.
10. De Mille, 179.
11. Graham, *Blood Memory*, 53.
12. De Mille, 182.
13. Stark Young, Dance Critic, *New Republic*, February 7, 1932.
14. Martin, Dance Critic, *New York Times*, February 8, 1931.

Chapter 6
1. De Mille, 211.
2. Graham, *Blood Memory*, 151.

Chapter 7
1. De Mille, 234.
2. Ibid., 236.
3. Graham, *Blood Memory*, 8.
4. Martha Graham, "Martha Graham Speaks," *Dance Observer*, April 1963, 54.
5. Ibid.
6. Martin Friedman, *Noguchi's Imaginary Landscape* (Minneapolis: Walker Art Center, 1978) as quoted in Ernestine Stodelle, *Deep Song: The Dance Story of Martha Graham* (New York: Macmillan, 1984), 132.
7. Graham, *Blood Memory*, 271.
8. Ibid., 266–267.
9. Jean Rosenthal and Lael Wertenbaker, *The Magic of Light* (Boston and Toronto: Little, Brown & Co., 1972), from Stodelle, 160.

Chapter 8
1. Terry, 113.
2. Ibid.
3. Ibid., 122.
4. McDonagh, 232.
5. De Mille, 314–315.

6. Graham, *Blood Memory*, 202.
7. Ibid., 203–204.

Chapter 9
1. Graham, *Blood Memory*, 202.
2. Stodelle, 179.
3. Terry, 118–119.
4. Martha Graham, "The Audacity of Performance," *Dance Magazine*, May 1953, 25.
5. Graham, *Blood Memory*, 210–211.
6. Graham, "Martha Graham Speaks," 53.
7. Tobi Tobias, "A Conversation with Martha Graham," *Dance Magazine*, March 1984, 64.
8. Graham, *Blood Memory*, 267.
9. Ibid., 258.
10. Ibid., 253.
11. Ibid., 251.
12. Ibid., 5.
13. Graham, "Martha Graham Speaks," 53.
14. Terry, 124.
15. Jennifer Dunning, "Martha Graham and Baryshnikov: Dynamics of a Simple Relationship," *New York Times*, October 14, 1991, Arts Sec. 1.
16. Graham, *Blood Memory*, 267.

Chapter 10
1. Graham, "Martha Graham Speaks," 54.

2. De Mille, 346.
3. De Mille, 362.
4. McDonagh, 289.
5. Graham, *Blood Memory*, 237.

Chapter 11

1. Martha Graham, interview by Mary Campbell, Associated Press Wire Service, June 17, 1975.
2. Dunning, "Martha Graham and Baryshnikov: Dynamics of a Simple Relationship," *New York Times*, October 14, 1991, Arts Sec. 1
3. Anna Kisselgoff, "A Martha Graham Student Comes Back," *New York Times*, June 12, 1975.
4. Jerry Parker, *Newsday*, June 20, 1975.
5. Murray Schumach, "Gala and Glamor Leap for Miss Graham," *New York Times*, June 20, 1975, Sec. 12.
6. Graham, *Blood Memory*, 170.
7. Tom Kerrigan, "Martha Graham: In Search of the Magic of Gesture, the Meaning of Movement," Martha Graham Dance Company Publicity Material, Nov. 24, 1975.
8. Eugenia Sheppard, "A Celebration of Firsts," Inside Fashion, *New York Post Magazine*, June 12, 1975, 7.

Chapter 12

1. Clive Barnes, "Graham: Growing Younger," *New York Post*, May 29, 1986.
2. Judith Michaelson, "Dance Community Split over Grant to Martha Graham," *Los Angeles Times*, July 25, 1988, Part VI.
3. Graham, *Blood Memory*, 270–271.
4. Ibid., 271.
5. Kisselgoff, "Reflections on Martha Graham's Revolution," *New York Times*, May 29, 1988, Sec. H6.
6. Jennifer Dunning, "Troupe Contemplates Life Without Graham," *New York Times*, April 3, 1991, Sec. C11.
7. Graham, *Blood Memory*, 262.
8. Dunning, "Troupe Contemplates Life Without Graham," *New York Times*, April 3, 1991, Sec. C11.
9. Janice Berman, "Martha Graham's Final Gift to Us," *Newsday*, June 5, 1991, Part II, 55.
10. Jennifer Dunning, "Martha Graham's Company Prepares for Her Centenary," *New York Times*, July 1, 1993, Sec. 12 C11.
11. Anna Kisselgoff, "Graham's Legacy: Consistent Change," *New York Times*, October 27, 1991, Sec. H.

For Further Reading

Armitage, Merle. *Martha Graham: The Early Years*. Los Angeles: Da Capo Press, 1937. Reprint paperback edition, 1978.

De Mille, Agnes. *Martha*. New York: Random House, 1991.

Graham, Martha. *Blood Memory*. New York: Doubleday, 1991.

————. *The Notebooks of Martha Graham*. New York: Harcourt, Brace, Jovanovich, 1973.

Horosko, Marian. *Martha Graham: The Evolution of Her Dance Theory and Training 1926–1991*. Chicago: Chicago Review Press, 1991.

McDonagh, Don. *Martha Graham: A Biography*. New York: Praeger, 1973.

Stodelle, Ernestine. *Deep Song: The Dance Story of Martha Graham*. New York: Macmillan, 1984.

Terry, Walter. *Frontiers of Dance: The Life of Martha Graham*. New York: Thomas Y. Crowell Company, 1975.

Index